T0286802

Cambridge Elements ☰

Elements in Second Language Acquisition
edited by
Alessandro G. Benati
University College Dublin
John W. Schwieter
Wilfrid Laurier University, Ontario

PRAGMATICS, GRAMMAR AND MEANING IN SLA

Aoife K. Ahern
Complutense University of Madrid

José Amenós-Pons
Complutense University of Madrid

Pedro Guijarro-Fuentes
University of the Balearic Islands

CAMBRIDGE
UNIVERSITY PRESS

Shaftesbury Road, Cambridge CB2 8EA, United Kingdom

One Liberty Plaza, 20th Floor, New York, NY 10006, USA

477 Williamstown Road, Port Melbourne, VIC 3207, Australia

314–321, 3rd Floor, Plot 3, Splendor Forum, Jasola District Centre,
New Delhi – 110025, India

103 Penang Road, #05–06/07, Visioncrest Commercial, Singapore 238467

Cambridge University Press is part of Cambridge University Press & Assessment,
a department of the University of Cambridge.

We share the University's mission to contribute to society through the pursuit of
education, learning and research at the highest international levels of excellence.

www.cambridge.org
Information on this title: www.cambridge.org/9781009507349

DOI: 10.1017/9781009026888

First published 2024

A catalogue record for this publication is available from the British Library.

ISBN 978-1-009-50734-9 Hardback
ISBN 978-1-009-01182-2 Paperback
ISSN 2517-7974 (online)
ISSN 2517-7966 (print)

Pragmatics, Grammar and Meaning in SLA

Elements in Second Language Acquisition

DOI: 10.1017/9781009026888
First published online: April 2024

Aoife K. Ahern
Complutense University of Madrid

José Amenós-Pons
Complutense University of Madrid

Pedro Guijarro-Fuentes
University of the Balearic Islands

Author for correspondence: Pedro Guijarro-Fuentes, p.guijarro@uib.es

Abstract: This Element explores the role of pragmatics, and its relationship with meaning and grammar, in second language acquisition. Specifically, this Element examines the generative paradigm, with its focus on purely linguistic aspects, in contrast with, and complemented by, the view of language adopted in the wider perspective on communication that Relevance Theory offers. It reviews several theoretical standpoints on how linguistic phenomena that require combining semantic, pragmatic and syntactic information are acquired and developed in second languages, illustrating how these perspectives are brought together in analysing data in different linguistic scenarios. It shows that the notion of procedural meaning casts light on the range of interpretative effects of grammatical features and how they vary across languages, suggesting ways to complete the picture of the interface factors that affect second language development.

Keywords: relevance theory, generative grammar, second language acquisition, pragmatics, semantics

ISBNs: 9781009507349 (HB), 9781009011822 (PB), 9781009026888 (OC)
ISSNs: 2517-7974 (online), 2517-7966 (print)

Contents

1 What Are the Key Concepts?

A fundamental question about the role of language in communication has been explored in a range of studies and with different purposes: is it more productive to study communication focusing on the meanings encoded in the words and phrases that we use, hear or read? Or should our priority be to better understand exactly how communication is made possible by inferring meanings that make sense in a given interaction or context, based on the words and phrases used? In other words, can communication be explained more fully and adequately through the study of semantics, or pragmatics?

In investigating second language acquisition (SLA), reflecting on this ques tion about the precise role of language in communication can lead to a way to frame our views of what language acquisition and learning consist of, as well as of the priorities for second language instruction. How important is it for learners to gain a functional command of the language, as opposed to prioritising accuracy in recognising and producing appropriate forms? To what extent will or should learners aspire to progressing further in their knowledge of the Second Language (L2) beyond the ability to engage in interaction that is 'good enough' to fulfil their immediate needs? What are the factors that spur this kind of progress towards high levels of competence – do they mainly depend on external help, guided practice and instruction, or depend above all on internal factors such as determination and metacognitive awareness for applying learning strategies?

From the perspective of generative grammar, what makes verbal communi-cation possible is linguistic competence: knowledge in the form of mental systems that develops based on an Universal Grammar (UG). Communication processes put the competence in action, so they are classified as performance, as opposed to competence. Of course, beyond linguistic competence, other kinds of knowledge are crucial in communication processes, including concepts of different kinds and socio-cultural knowledge. Effective use of language to communicate, that is producing and understanding discourse sequences and their relevance within a specific situation, involves orchestrating the mental processing of this wide range of kinds of knowledge, bringing them together so that they connect at what are known as *interfaces*: points of contact between, for example, encoded meaning (semantics), the speaker's purpose and the situation (pragmatics), or grammatical structure (syntax) and intonation (prosody).

Considering language processing and language acquisition as products of the human mind, in which linguistic competence must interact with other cognitive capacities, in this book we will explore how a cognitive pragmatic theory like Relevance Theory (RT) offers potential venues for explaining different kinds of processing challenges, related to the interfaces, in the acquisition of additional languages. This will also allow us to reflect on how compatible the assumptions of the two frameworks are, and on the potential of combining notions and approaches from each of them in ways that can contribute to understanding, explaining and perhaps improving teaching to enhance SLA processes.

In relation to these aims, in the next section we will move on to introduce specific concepts from Generative (mainly Minimalist) Grammar and from RT. The mutual interplay of these concepts and the ways that they can serve as analytical tools will progressively be developed and discussed in the following sections.

1.1 Pragmatics and Cognitive Pragmatics

Pragmatics is the study of how communication works and more specifically of the role of the array of sources of information that contribute to communication alongside language itself. Pragmatics is also a perspective from which to contemplate linguistic phenomena: it starts from the data offered by the linguistic system and takes into consideration the extralinguistic elements that condition the interpretation of these data.

Therefore, as communication takes place in socially grounded situations among agents who take part in interaction, pragmatics inevitably includes the analysis of social factors and the external circumstances in which all communicative processes are framed. Yet meanwhile, in order for communication to be effective, the participants (communicators and addressees) engage in certain ways of behaving, and an ample body of research and thought has been dedicated to identifying the principles that form the basis of efficient communicative behaviour (e.g., from speech act theory (Austin, 1962; Searle, 1969) to Grice's (1975) maxims of conversation or neo-Gricean theorists (Horn, 1984; Levinson, 1995, 2000). These principles can be seen as assumptions upon which we humans base the mental operations involved in producing and interpreting messages. Thus, for instance, we assume that when someone produces a message by saying something or writing it, they communicate in a cooperative manner.

The work of H.P. Grice, and in particular his well-known theory of implicature, cooperative principle and maxims of conversation (Grice, 1975), were ground-breaking for the study of verbal communication. They shed light on the deductive, inferential processes involved in interpreting, based on what the speaker says and the communicative situation, what the speaker's intended meaning is.

Building upon the seminal works of Grice, over the decades of the late twentieth and early twenty-first centuries, researchers known as Neo-Gricean (see, in particular, Horn, 1984, 1989, 2004; Levinson, 1987a and b, 1991, 2000) further developed the study of implicature. The developments include pinpointing the format in which the link between linguistic form and interpretation exists. To exemplify this point, let us imagine an utterance such as:

(1)   Let's play that again.

If it is said, for instance, (a) by a person holding a guitar after finishing a song, (b) by a child to her friend when they see a board game on a shelf at home, or (c) by an orchestra conductor standing in front of an ensemble after they have played a piece, the interpretation will vary. The referent of the subject of 'play' will differ; it includes the speaker and the addressee(s), so it depends on who speaks and who is the hearer. Likewise, the interpretation of the verb 'play' will be 'perform music' or 'take part in a game'. In situation (c), the semantically encoded meaning of 'play' will be adjusted to include 'direct the performance of music'. In sum, examining the variability of interpretations that are possible for a given phrase or sentence requires considering different aspects of the communicative situation it is uttered in. This kind of variation in the way a single phrase or sentence can be interpreted is not at all an exception; interpretation is always reliant on contextual factors. Thus, in the search for how to account for the dynamic interaction between meaning and context, what is known as the cognitive turn in pragmatics has led to substantial progress. In this tradition, researchers have identified the key component that makes it possible to explain how such diverse elements become involved in the interpretation of linguistic expressions: they must take on the form of mental representations, the link between linguistic form and interpretation.

In the works of Grice and the Neo-Gricean, references to the processes of interpretation are constant. Typically, however, these theories take a philosophical approach to the study of language in use, rather than attempt to offer a psychologically plausible description of the processes they describe. In this sense, they cannot be considered cognitive approaches to pragmatics, although Grice's ideas are the starting point for such approaches.

Thus, cognitive pragmatics can be defined as any approach to pragmatics that focuses on the cognitive aspects of the construal of meaning in context (Schmid, 2012, p. 3). This kind of approach does not exclude the analysis of language or the study of the semantics of linguistic expressions, but it situates language and linguistic semantics within a general conception of human communication and cognition.

From the point of view of cognitive pragmatics, in addition to the principles that guide communicative processes, the social and physical circumstances in which these take place are all considered in the light of how they are represented in the minds of the participants in a communicative process. Therefore, this might be seen as a field that attempts to generalise about what seems to be exactly that which is ungeneralisable, since what is context-dependent must be unpredictable; and cognitive processes, given that they take place in individual minds, will tend to be idiosyncratic and particular. Yet from the perspective adopted herein, we will consider both kinds of generalisations – those about language itself, as well as about how communicative context affects the ways that it is used and interpreted – to not only be possible, but also particularly useful. We hope to show how these generalisations can be applied in extending and deepening our understanding of how linguistic and extralinguistic aspects of communication are inextricable and essential components in explaining many aspects of how language is used and therefore, how it conveys meaning, and are helpful for language instructors and learners to be aware of.

When a speaker or writer produces any linguistic expression, it is known as an utterance. To explore the respective roles of meaning (semantically encoded) as opposed to the interpretation of utterances, the perspective of cognitive pragmatics considers all the different kinds of factors that influence how we understand what a speaker means as useful for analysis inasmuch as the participants in communication have access to them in the form of mental representations. Stereotypical examples of the differences between 'semantic' or literal meaning and pragmatic meaning or, as more clearly defined by Grice, speaker meaning (i.e., what a speaker intends to convey) include, for example, using *can you pass the salt?* as a request or even – using particular intonation and rhythm – an order. Speakers of many languages use an equivalent expression (words with the same meaning) for the same purpose. But the success of using this expression for the usual purpose depends on the hearer's association between the linguistic forms and the speaker's intent. This is so because relying on the literal, 'semantic' meaning of the words used, and excluding the contextual factors, would lead to understanding this utterance to be a question about the hearer's capabilities.

The 'pass the salt' example (as in *can you pass me the salt?)* is typical in speech act theory discussions, in which the use of utterances to perform different kinds of actions is analysed; in this case, the use of a question (about the hearer's ability) to politely request the hearer to do something. Speech act theorists (such as Austin, 1962 and Searle, 1972) focused their attention on the external conditions that determine which linguistic expressions are more appropriate for what the communicator intends to do by means of saying something. However, the connection between such external conditions – for instance, with the salt example, that the interaction takes place in a situation in which the hearer can easily carry out the action (e.g., the salt is within their reach) – and the literal meaning of the words used lies beyond these authors' main concerns. As Grice later came to explain, the connection relies on our inferential reasoning, which we perform based on shared expectations and assumptions about how conversation works.

In sum, cognitive pragmatics constitutes a perspective that assumes that all the information that is accessed when interpreting utterances must exist in the form of mental representations that are accessible to the hearer or reader. Our perceptions of the socio-physical environment, the identities of those involved in a communicative exchange, as well as the assumptions that we access, all form part of the cognitive environment which we rely on to make sense of what is said. In this way, cognitive pragmatics has provided the potential means for a plausible explanation of the processes by which such a varied range of kinds of information can be taken into account and interact with linguistic meaning in communication.

1.2 Relevance Theory

The most prominent representative of cognitive pragmatics is Dan Sperber and Deirdre Wilson's (1986/95) RT. RT is a theory about human communication that focuses on the interpretation of utterances. Building upon Grice's theory of implicature and maxims of conversation, Sperber and Wilson highlight the ostensive-inferential nature of verbal communication. They argue that by performing an ostensive act, we convey to our audience our intention that they will acquire relevant information, while simultaneously conveying the information itself. Assuming that human cognition is optimised for 'improving the quantity, quality and organization of the individual's knowledge' (Sperber and Wilson, 1987, p. 669), when we are aware that a stimulus is presented to us ostensively, as occurs in all communicative acts, an automatic, unconscious process of inferential interpretation is triggered. This response is based on the presumption of optimal relevance that characterises any ostensive act:

(a) The ostensive stimulus is relevant enough for it to be worth the addressee's effort to process it.
(b) The ostensive stimulus is the most relevant one compatible with the communicator's abilities and preferences (Sperber and Wilson, 1995, pp. 266–278).

Ostensive-inferential communication involves interpreting utterances following the communicative principle of relevance, by which hearers identify the speaker's meaning as the one that provides the most cognitive effects in relation to the processing effort required to interpret it. The central claims of this theory include the two principles of relevance:

- The cognitive principle: Human cognition tends to be geared to the maximisation of relevance.
- The communicative principle: Every utterance conveys a presumption of its own optimal relevance.

Among the interesting advantages of this theory is the fact that it allows for a rational delimitation of the labour of semantics, namely, to identify linguistically encoded meaning, as opposed to pragmatics, which has the goal of describing the processes by which the speaker's intended meaning is identified through decoding and inference.

The RT view of utterance interpretation is that all verbal communication involves the use of encoded linguistic meaning as an indication of what the speaker intends to convey. Yet the presumption of optimal relevance leads hearers to using contextual information to identifying not only the meaning of the words that have been used but also what the speaker meaning is and the implications of the utterance. Hence, in (2), what the hearer knows about the communicative situation will determine the meaning they attribute to the speaker's intention.

(2)   Ana: Shall we go for a walk?
        Bruno: The park's closed.

If Bruno and Ana usually walk in the local park, Ana will probably infer that Bruno is rejecting her suggestion to take a walk together. The inferential process by which she would reach that conclusion would involve considering the premises that (a) Bruno usually walks in the park, and (b) Bruno affirms the park's closed, and therefore, he is responding to her suggestion by showing that there's a good reason why they cannot take their usual walk, so he won't go for a walk.

If the circumstances were, instead, that the two interlocutors usually go walking by the river when the park is closed, Ana would not probably take Bruno's words as an answer to her invitation, and she would probably interpret that Bruno accepts her suggestion and will go for a walk. On the RT view, interpreting any utterance requires pragmatic inference, since contextual information is necessary to identify all aspects of meaning, including literal meaning that is identified by decoding. The referent of the pronoun 'we' in Ana's utterance requires accessing information about who the speaker is and who she includes as the other individual's referred to by the plural form of this pronoun, in this case herself and the hearer, Bruno. On the other hand, in identifying the relevant interpretation of Bruno's utterance in response to her suggestion, it is also necessary not only to identify the intended referent, for instance, of 'the park' as being the local park where they sometimes walk, but also to reason about why Bruno affirms what he does. This requires knowledge about the communicative situation, the speaker and hearer's relationship, as well as knowing that they sometimes go for walks and where they do this, all of which would be accessed to interpret his response to the suggestion – whether he accepts or rejects it.

Thus, as mentioned in the previous section, when interpreting an utterance, we take into account an array of different kinds of information; information that is integrated into inferential processes is accessed in the form of mental representations. In this sense, RT is a cognitive theory of pragmatics. It describes how the characteristics of human beings' cognitive systems lead us to behave in rational, predictable ways when we engage in communication. In other words, as highlighted by Sperber and Wilson (1995, p. 271), the communicative principle of relevance makes 'a descriptive not a normative claim about the content of a given act of ostensive communication'. Likewise, the presumption of optimal relevance describes an inherent quality of ostensive-inferential acts, not a goal that should be achieved.

In their substantial body of work, and the work of many other researchers, Sperber and Wilson's original theory has provided a framework for the analysis of the processes of ostensive-inferential communication. On the RT view, the role of encoded meaning within verbal communication leads to a schematic representation of the proposition expressed, known within RT as a conceptual representation. The conceptual representation that is derived from the encoded meaning of the expressions used in an utterance is called the explicature.

In identifying the explicature of an utterance, the hearer (hereon, hearer will be used in place of hearer or reader) accesses three kinds of information in order to identify the concepts that are conveyed: logical, encyclopaedic and lexical information. The explicature of an utterance is the development of the linguistically encoded logical form (LF) of the sentences (or the string of words) being used. Determining the explicature of *The park is closed* is not only a matter of decoding: it also involves reference assignment (Which park is referred in the utterance? and When is it closed?) and semantic disambiguation (Which of the meanings of the word 'close' needs to be accessed to interpret the sentence?). Therefore, pragmatics plays a decisive role in determining the proposition expressed, along with semantics and syntax.

In RT, a further difference is established between basic-level explicatures and higher-level explicatures. Reference assignment and semantic disambiguation allow the hearer to recover the basic explicature. However, in the above example, understanding that Bruno's utterance is a rejection (or alternatively, an acceptation) implies recognizing the intended speech act. Developing 'The park is closed' as 'The speaker does not want to go for a walk' implies determining the higher-level explicature, that is, something that Bruno intended to communicate by uttering his words.

However, in our example, the interpretation process will not stop there. By comparing Bruno's current answer to previous experiences of verbal interaction with him, Ana might conclude that Bruno is replying dryly; she will then access background information about Bruno's circumstances and might decide that he is worried about a person he loves, or about a job he is about to lose. The interpretation will then be: 'Bruno does not want to go for a walk because he is seriously worried about his mother/his job/ . . . '. Ana might also conclude that Bruno's intention was for her to realise that he was worried but did not want to talk about it. The reason why Bruno did not want to go for a walk nor have a friendly conversation, and the fact that he intended Ana to realise that he was worried but did not want to talk about it, is a set of communicated implications that do not rely on (linguistically or otherwise) coded content. Within RT, this kind of communicated implication is called an *implicature*. Implicatures are strongly implicated when it is necessary to access them to reach a relevant interpretation of the utterance, while they can be weak implicatures if they are accessible based on the utterance and context, but not necessary to identify a relevant interpretation.

1.3 Linguistic Meaning and Linguistic Underdetermination in RT

RT differentiates two types of linguistic meaning (Blakemore, 1987; Wilson and Sperber, 1993): on the one hand, the meaning of expressions that encode concepts; on the other hand, that of expressions whose contribution consists of guiding the addressee's inferences, restricting the way in which the conceptual contents of the utterance should be related, or making certain assumptions or implicatures more accessible as part of the inferential process. Conceptual and procedural expressions have different properties: conceptual meaning is accessible to introspection and awareness, that is, any speaker can explain (with more or less precision) the meaning of conceptual expressions. In contrast, procedural meaning is much more abstract, barely accessible to introspection and difficult to verbalise.

Blakemore's (1987) initial proposal on this distinction suggested that the conceptual–procedural divide coincides with the distinction between truth-conditional and non-truth-conditional meaning (where truth-conditional meaning contributes to the proposition expressed by an utterance, and hence to its speech-act content, and non-truth-conditional meaning constrains the inferential phases of comprehension). But Wilson and Sperber (1993) reassessed this distinction, arguing that (a) not all conceptual expressions are truth-conditional, (b) not all procedural expressions are non-truth-conditional and (c) not all procedural expressions impose constraints on the construction of contexts and cognitive effects.

The conceptual–procedural distinction has been extensively developed by relevance theorists and applied in differing ways in a wide range of languages (cf. Escandell-Vidal, Leonetti and Ahern, 2011). Here we will focus on the proposals by Escandell-Vidal (2000) and Escandell and Leonetti (2011, 2012), since they establish a direct and explicit relationship between this distinction and the theoretical framework of generative grammar. To a large extent, these authors assimilate the dichotomy between conceptual categories and procedural categories with the generativist dichotomy *lexical* versus *functional* categories. Thus, linguistic expressions with functional meaning (articles, pronouns, verbal morphemes and many discourse connectives) are considered procedural, while content words (nouns, adjectives, verbs and most adverbs) are conceptual. The identification, however, is not total, since the grammatical distinction has a syntactic nature, while the RT proposal emphasises the differing contributions of each category to the processes of utterance interpretation.

On Escandell-Vidal and Leonetti's view, procedural meaning is both rigid and schematic: thus, features encoded by inflectional morphology are invariable, always contributing a single, semantically encoded indication that operates on inferential interpretation processes. Nevertheless, these features underdetermine the potential interpretations the expression can lead to. Hence, a procedural expression, despite its specific and invariable meaning, can give rise to a wide range of interpretations depending on the discourse environment the mental representations activated when building the context. In contrast, conceptual meanings are much more flexible and adaptable depending on specific interpretive needs.

RT adheres to what is known as the linguistic underdetermination thesis. According to this thesis, the (conceptual or procedural) semantics of natural language expressions do not fully determine what is said. Languages can thus be seen as mechanisms that produce strings of symbols, in which forms and meanings are conventionally and systematically associated. But when used in communication, speakers exploit the reactive and activating potential of linguistic expressions and employ them as cues pointing to a wider set of representations. What is communicated is not only a set of conventional associations of form-meaning relations, but an assembly of contextually enriched data to be completed and transformed (Escandell-Vidal, 2020, p. 42).

1.4 Modularity of Mind

RT is built upon a modular conception of the human mind, initially inspired by Fodor's (1983) theories. Fodor himself drew on Chomsky's postulates on the architecture of the mind: the basic idea is that the human mind possesses a set of modules specialised in performing specific functions. Thus, the mind is 'compartmentalised' into units, and each one is dedicated to the processing of a specific type of input (e.g., visual processing from visual stimuli).

Fodor argues that, alongside the specialised modules, there is a central system that harmonises their functioning. However, the existence of this central system has been questioned in more recent research, giving rise to the *massive modularity* hypothesis (Sperber, 1994, 2002, 2005; Carruthers, 2006). RT identifies a cognitive module for comprehension (Sperber, 2005; Sperber and Wilson, 2002, 2005; Mercier and Sperber, 2011, 2017; Wilson, 2000/2012, 2017; Wilson and Sperber, 2002, 2004), resulting from the evolution from a more general mind-reading module (Sperber, 1996, 2000, 2002; Origgi and Sperber, 2000; Wilson, 2000/2012; Sperber and Wilson, 2002, 2004; Wilson, 2017). Furthermore, RT predicts the existence of modules for emotion reading (Carston, 2016; Wilson, 2011, 2016), for speech production and syntax (Levelt, 1993), for epistemic vigilance (Sperber et al., 2010), for argumentation (Mercier and Sperber, 2011, 2017) and for social cognition (Happé et al., 2017). These modules are oriented towards obtaining the maximum cognitive benefit in exchange for the minimum processing effort. Modules take as input the output of other modules and their processing results in interpretive hypotheses about the speaker's meaning and intentions (Wilson, 2005; Figueras, 2020).

1.5 Linguistic Interfaces

Most approaches to language cognition make strong theoretical predictions for close connections between language acquisition and the emergence of complex properties that characterise and distinguish human languages across space and time (see e.g., Chomsky, 2007; O'Grady, 2005 a and b; Jackendoff, 2002; Tomasello, 2003, 2008). The studying of sub-parts of grammatical systems in isolation (e.g., phonology, syntax, semantics and morphology) cannot provide us with explanatorily adequate answers to primary questions such as what constitutes linguistic knowledge or how it is acquired. A non-combined approach – focusing on just one of these systems – might be able to meet the weight of descriptive adequacy for specific, narrow questions. However, only a fully integrated approach, involving the study of the interaction between different levels of linguistic knowledge and their interaction with non-linguistic cognitive and spatial domains, known as *interfaces*, offers promise for shedding light on these fundamental questions (e.g., Chomsky, 1995; Jackendoff, 2002).

Chomsky's (1995) Minimalist Program (MP) views language as constrained to a set of core competencies, instantiated as a computational mechanism. This mechanism is contended to be universal, which suggests, in turn, that the actual locus of most language acquisition processes should take place at the interfaces, that is, the points of connection, between cognitive modules. When acquiring languages, then, the exposure the learners experience is what constitutes the primary linguistic data that their cognitive processing resources work on. Exactly what the learner acquires from all these data will depend not only on the individual's cognitive resources, but also on how frequent and how salient the words, expressions and structures are in the input that they hear and read.

There are different views of exactly what the term *interface* refers to. This term has been used to refer, in the literature, to a particular shared understanding of how language and cognition are represented in the mind, or to how mental computation, processing and performance of language work together.

Chomsky (1995) focuses on the idea of interfaces as representational components. However, Jackendoff (2002) developed a detailed, influential proposal of how the modular structure of language manages language stimuli. He distinguished *integrative* (modular) as opposed to *interface* linguistic processes, formulating an interface-conditioned view of interaction between internal and external modules.

In a rupture from more traditional generative theorizing where syntax was always taken to be the sole central component of language, Jackendoff (2002) proposes an architecture for language that distances itself from what he regards the 'syntactocentrism' of all previous standard generative models. On his view, phonology (PF, Phonetic Form) and meaning (LF, Logical Form) were always treated as being derived from syntax to a greater or lesser degree, even in the most recent instantiations of the framework: the MP (Chomsky, 1995). In most typical models associated with the MP, linguistic derivations continue to split, leading in one direction for phonological spell-out (to PF) and in another direction for semantic computation (to LF) after movement, Merge and Agree operations unite lexical items according to their associated intrinsic lexical constraints.

In discarding the notion that syntax is the sole central combinatorial system, Jackendoff offers the alternative that 'language comprises a number of independent combinatorial systems, which are aligned with each other by means of a collection of interface systems. Syntax is among the combinatorial systems, but far from the only one' (Jackendoff, 2002, p. 111). This model of interfaces (for more information on this concept, see Section 2) consigns conceptual structure at one end of the continuum, and phonological structure at the other, with syntax remaining between. Hence, in this system, there is a perfect division between integrative and interface linguistic processes, whereby conceptual structure interfaces with perception and action, phonology with hearing and speech production.

Related to the increasing significance of interfaces in theoretical linguistics, formal acquisition theorizing has placed a greater empirical emphasis on studying the acquisition of properties that are interface-conditioned. Under the hypothesis that such properties, as compared against truly integrative properties – especially those strictly captured within the computational system-, are more difficult to acquire a priori, interface properties are predicted to take longer to acquire. They might be subject to very long-lasting delays and perhaps non-convergence in bilingualism in child and adult acquisition alike; in other words, it is possible that some of these properties are not fully acquired at all by non-native speakers (e.g., Sorace, 2011, 2012). The role of interface phenomena is highlighted in specific theoretical models of language processing, such as the Modular Cognition Framework (Sharwood Smith and Truscott, 2014; Truscott, 2015; Sharwood Smith, 2017; Truscott and Sharwood Smith, 2019; Truscott, 2022) (see Section 2.3).

1.6 Principles and Parameters

Principles and parameters are two categories that form part of the theory of UG; in Chomsky's Minimalist Program (1995), these categories make it possible to explain the concept of linguistic competence. The principles refer to the general properties of human language; they are abstract, common to all languages (therefore, universal) and innate (White, 1989). On the other hand, parameters refer to the different options that each language adopts; they are specific, particular to each language, and learned. Principles and parameters are purely linguistic (mainly morphosyntactic) notions; they are needed to understand how language structures (i.e., strings of linguistic symbols) are produced, in which forms and meanings are conventionally and systematically associated in discourse. Therefore, they are the basis of pragmatic phenomena found in verbal communication.

A parameter is, thus, the degree of variation that a linguistic universal admits in each of its particular realisations. The particular values of each parameter in a given language are fixed in childhood during the acquisition process.

As for principles, some of them are of a fixed nature. For example, the 'principle of structural dependency' establishes that in all languages the relationship between the different components of a sentence depends on a hierarchical structure, not on the sequence in which they appear. This principle can admit certain degrees of variation in its expression in the different particular languages: in some languages, adjectives can be placed before or after the noun, while others require adjectives to appear in a certain position; Spanish admits adjectives before and after the noun, although with a different meaning in each case (Demonte, 2008).

Another characteristic of parameters is that, in some cases, there is a contrast between an unmarked option and a marked one. This is the case, for example, of the Null Subject, or Pro-drop, Parameter. In pro-drop languages (such as Spanish *Comí allí* 'I ate there' and not necessarily *Yo comí allí* 'I ate there') this is an unmarked parameter, which allows omitting the subject of the sentence; other languages have this parameter marked, which prevents deletion of the subject.

The unmarked option represents the initial value within the UG system. In contrast, the marked option is only accessed thanks to the input data that the person receives during their learning process (Liceras, 1996). Accordingly, each parameter consists of an initial fixation (i.e., setting), which is not marked, and successive marked fixations. In this way, the UG is structured in a nuclear grammar and a peripheral grammar. The core grammar contains the unmarked fixations of general parameters and principles. The peripheral grammar contains marked fixations, specific to each language and learned through experience. From the point of view of SLA, this parameter-marking hypothesis offers interesting advantages for explaining the learning process. If a parameter has been set with the same option of being marked, or not being marked, in both of the languages the learner is exposed to (L1, L2 and Ln), then they will have no difficulty learning the L2. If the option is different in each language, the situation varies according to the direction of the itinerary between the language with the option marked and the one language in which it is not marked: learning will be more difficult in the case that L2 has the option marked, and easier if it is unchecked (White, 1989).

1.7 Features

The term *feature*, in a broad sense, can be defined as a basic or elementary piece of linguistic information, whether phonological, morphological, syntactic or lexical. Features are combined in a restricted and articulated way and give rise to linguistic segments of varying complexity. In this section, only syntactic features will be dealt with. Thus, in a stricter and more technical sense, which is the one used in generative grammar, the term feature encompasses the syntactic notions necessary to characterise functional units (words or morphemes), and especially to account for the processes of agreement and movement, together with those that make it possible to establish relations of quantification,

Table 1 Gender and aspect features contrasted across languages.

Feature	Language A	Language B
GENDER	French: la table (fem) le pouvoir (masc)	German: die Katze (fem) der Hunde (masc) das Haus (neutral)
ASPECT	Mandarin Chinese: 我吃过饭了 (Wǒ chī guò fàn le) I have eaten (perfect) 我正在吃饭 (Wǒ zhèngzài chī fàn) I am eating (progressive)	Russian: Я читаю книгу (Ya chitayu knigu) I am reading a book (present tense, ongoing action; imperfective) Я прочитал книгу (Ya prochital knigu) I have read the book (past tense, completed action; perfect)
	Mandarin lacks verb forms that encode imperfect aspect.	Russian does not have forms that encode progressive aspect.

reference, subordination, determination, etc. (Chomsky, 1995; Borer, 2003; Adger and Svenonius, 2011; Bosque, 2016; Adger, 2021; Svenonius, 2021; among others). In RT-oriented approaches to linguistic analysis, features have been used to characterise the semantics of linguistic expressions, which underlie the contextual enrichment potentialities of any expression (Escandell-Vidal, 2010, 2016; Escandell-Vidal and Leonetti, 2011).

In formal linguistics, features are seen as values taken by a property or attribute. For example, for the property GENDER, in some languages (such as Romance languages) there are two possible values: masculine and feminine. In other languages (for example, in German), however, the property GENDER can also have a neutral value. Similarly, the ASPECT property may be perfective or imperfective in some languages, while in others there will be further relevant values, such as perfect or progressive (see examples in Table 1).

In generative grammar, it is common to represent features as sets of binary options (Adger, 1993). For example, ASPECT is often represented as [±perfective]. The – (minus) option may be subject to further specification, implying the idea that, at least in some cases, there is an implicative hierarchy of grammatical features (Clements, 1985; Archangeli, 1988; Clements and Hume, 1995).[1]

---

[1] However, there are other ways of representing features, without necessarily implying a hierarchy of binary options: the formula [ATTRIBUTE: value], as in [GENDER: masculine] or [ASPECT: perfective], is a representational alternative that does not presuppose a particular number of values or a particular hierarchy.

Not all properties can be encoded or described as a linguistic feature, but only those that have syntactic or morphological consequences. Conversely, semantic or encyclopaedic aspects that may be relevant for the description of objects in the world, but not for the characterisation of strictly linguistic properties, are not considered as a linguistic feature. Although this general idea is usually accepted, in practice there is no consensus on the (more or less) restrictive boundaries of the concept. For example, in many studies on clitic pronouns, among other semantic features the existence of the feature [±specificity] is accepted (Suñer, 1988; Sportiche, 1996); however, Leonetti (2004, 2007, 2012) argues that specificity is not properly a feature, but a semantic-pragmatic notion that derives (in certain settings) from the feature [±defined]. For Borer (2003), features articulate not only syntactic processes, but also the meanings of lexical items and sentences; even interface levels of representation contain nothing more than sets of lexical features (Baker, 2008; Borer, 2003). In contrast, in approaches that give greater prominence to pragmatics (for instance, Leonetti's 2007), the number of features tends to be reduced and certain information is attributed to inferential mechanisms operating at the syntax/ semantics/pragmatics interfaces.

Words are not marked with individual, isolated features; features form *clusters* or *bundles*. Thus, features constitute particular bundles which vary according to various factors, subject to hierarchies. For example, personal pronouns are usually made up of a particular bundle of features: PERSON, GENDER, NUMBER and CASE. Other features are occasionally added, such as REFLEXIVITY (Bosque, 2016, p. 325). In many cases, there is variation in the bundles of features encoded in an expression in one language and its equivalent in another language. There are also differences in the features of the expressions that convey certain meanings in different languages, that is, two languages may use different grammatical categories (nouns, verbs, and so on) to express the same meaning. The way in which features are grouped in each language is a fundamental factor of variation. In addition, variation is found in how features are organised in bundles, but also which features are active within one specific language as opposed to another (for the consequences of this for L2 acquisition, see the section on *Feature Reassembly Hypothesis* (FRH) in Section 2).

Grammatical features can be classified according to different criteria. In the previous paragraph, for example, the concept of categorical features was evoked; such features allow us to establish word categories (article, adjective, pronoun, verb, and so on). In turn, word categories can be grouped into two types: lexical and functional categories. Lexical categories form open paradigms (nouns, verbs, adjectives and adverbs) and have descriptive content (in RT terms, conceptual meaning); functional categories form closed paradigms (determiners, prepositions, conjunctions and inflectional informa-tion) and do not have descriptive content; rather, their semantics is established using a set of abstract grammar-internal notions: reference, determination, comparison, predication, person, number, tense, perfectivity, and so on (in RT, functional categories are considered to have procedural meaning).

In generative grammar, features are also classified according to the type of contribution they make to meaning. Thus, there exists a contrast between interpretable and non-interpretable features (Chomsky, 1995); interpretable features are those which provide information relevant to the conceptual-intentional system, that is, to language expressing referential meaning; while non-interpretable features provide information relevant only to the determination of syntactic relations within the sentence, and more specifically, agreement or concord processes (Chomsky, 2000, 2001). For example, in Romance languages, determiners and adjectives incorporate gender and num-ber marking, that is, they agree in gender and number with the noun they accompany. This helps establish the internal relations and boundaries of the noun phrase, but the only gender and number marks on the noun constitute interpretable features. Similarly, the verb tenses of Romance languages (unlike English) incorporate a person feature, but it is not interpretable, since it is a syntactic feature intended to establish agreement with the person feature of the subject.

2 What Are the Main Branches of Research?

Following on from some of the basic concepts introduced in the previous section, this section delves further into some of them, particularly considering RT and SLA and some of the UG constructs. We have seen how RT focuses on processes of interpretation that go beyond the ones involved in linguistic coding and decoding, adopting a view of communication as an ostensive-inferential process. RT upholds that the output of the purely linguistic processing mechan-isms is formed not only by accessing linguistic representations, but also through pragmatic inferencing in order to identify meaning. In addition, it was shown how procedural encoding affects the inferential processes and the contextual assumptions accessed in syntactic parsing. That is, despite forming part of the purely linguistic mechanisms of the phonological and syntactic modules, pro-cedural expressions are related to pragmatics, because they restrict inferential, extralinguistic processing that is involved in identifying speaker meaning.

So, in relation to our goal of identifying some aspects of what RT can offer for understanding SLA processes, we provide here some background on current views of the development of grammatical competence. These views examine the roles of the subpersonal (i.e., consciously inaccessible) mental systems that characterise syntactic processing – and also pragmatic processing – how they interact at the interfaces with other cognitive modules, and hypothesise about their development in SLA.

2.1 UG and SLA

Within the framework of generative grammar, the concept of UG is a fundamental one in describing and analysing language competence and language acquisition. UG consists of the set of principles, rules and conditions that all languages share. This concept constitutes the nucleus of the theory of generative-transformational grammar, with which Chomsky proposed to explain the processes of acquisition and use of language. According to this theory, all human beings naturally acquire any language because they have an innate, specifically human capacity in the form of a UG. This capacity, independent of all other human capacities, manifests itself in the form of universal knowledge about the properties common to all languages and the specific features of each one.

On Chomsky's view, speakers access the content of UG through the activation of the language acquisition device (LAD). Acquiring a language, therefore, consists of learning to apply universal principles to the language in question and identifying the appropriate value of each of the parameters. Since the publication of Syntactic Structures (Chomsky, 1957), which is considered the beginning of generativism or generative-transformational grammar, this theory has undergone successive reformulations until the arrival of the MP (Chomsky, 1995). With the UG hypothesis, Chomsky intends to solve the 'logical problem of language acquisition' or 'learnability problem', that is, to explain how the speaker can acquire language in a relatively short period of time, overcoming the deficiencies of the input they receive. This problem is known as the 'poverty of the input'. The assumption that input gives rise to acquisition by itself is considered problematic because, on the one hand, the language input people are exposed to contains elements of linguistic performance that hinder acquisition (e.g., false principles, errors, ungrammatical expressions and so on). On the other hand, it is problematic because the input never offers information about the deficient, erroneous or ungrammatical nature of language performance, which would prevent the individual from identifying ungrammatical elements. The explanation that Chomsky gives of this process is precisely that the use of UG allows the individual to select the adequate input and learn the particular rules of the language in question.

Chomsky's theory has, nevertheless, received some criticism, especially in certain partial aspects. One of them is the speed with which Chomsky claims that language acquisition occurs. According to some studies, children spend much more time acquiring language than Chomsky claimed, and the process is developed with greater intensity than he suggested. Another is the innate nature of certain syntactic principles, which is not considered sufficiently established. Finally, the poverty of the stimulus factor does not seem to require the hypothesis of a UG.

Leaving aside these critiques, within the approaches to applying the Chomskyan framework to research on SLA, three types of accounts can be distinguished regarding the role of UG (White, 2003 and references therein): (a) there is no difference in the use of UG, whether it is an L1 or an L2; (b) for L2 learners, especially adults, it is impossible to access UG and (c) UG is one of the factors involved in the acquisition and learning process of an L2, but not the only one.

With this preamble in mind, over the years, the study of SLA (as well as L1 acquisition and other language acquisition scenarios) has moved from the Principles and Parameters framework (Chomsky, 1981) to the MP (Chomsky, 1995, 2001 and thereafter). In other words, previous accounts based on Principles and Parameters have fallen out of favour against Minimalist theorizing and other theoretical frameworks (Lardiere, 2008, 2009; Slabakova et al., 2014 and references thereafter). That (inter)language variation can be more aptly explained by appealing to cross-linguistic differences outside syntactic parameters is by now unquestionable; variation in the lexicon, types of features, feature bundles which are not part of the syntactic core system proper can clearly all contribute to answering the logical problem of language acquisition.

The learning task of any adult L2 learner is, thus, in principle not so different from that of an L1 child. Namely, in order for an adult L2 learner to converge on the target representation of any given L2, they must have access to the UG features that remained present, albeit unspecified, during the course of L1 acquisition. However, there are many more internal and external factors involved in adult language learning, not the least that the initial state of acquisition is different from that of the child. With this in mind, current SLA research within the generative approach aims to tease apart two notable Minimalism-informed hypotheses with a focus on the role of interpretable and uninterpretable features in SLA, namely the *Interpretability Hypothesis* (Hawkins and Hattori, 2006; Tsimpli and Dimitrakopoulou, 2007) and the *Feature Reassembly Hypothesis* (Lardiere, 2008, 2009 and references thereafter). In so doing, current research attempts to provide an answer to the question of how morphological variability and convergence of L2 grammars can be properly accounted for by testing grammatical structures of differential complexity involving (un-)interpretable features.

Even within Minimalist theorising, one central question that remains is that of the lasting function of UG with particular reference to the so-called critical period (Lenneberg, 1967). Some have argued that UG, as a superset of all possible formal grammatical features in a given natural language, is no longer – or only partially – available to adults in the same way as it is to child language learners. These perspectives are also known as partial-access theories (Clahsen and Muysken, 1986; Schachter, 1989; Hawkins and Chan, 1997; Hawkins and Hattori, 2006; Tsimpli and Dimitrakopoulou, 2007; Tsimpli and Mastropavlou, 2008). In contrast, Full Access approaches (e.g. Epstein, Flynn and Martohardjono, 1996; Schwartz and Sprouse, 1996; White, 2003, to name just a few) differ in the way UG constrains the development of interlanguage (L2) grammars. They presuppose that L2 learners have access to the complete inventory of UG features (together with related syntactic operations and principles) without being affected by any restrictions imposed by a critical period. Notably, Full Access approaches uphold that native-like grammar representations are indeed possible in L2 syntax despite poverty of the stimulus (Chomsky, 1982). In other words, L2 learners can attain complex and subtle properties of language that could not have been generated from the L2 input received (White, 2003 and references thereafter).

2.2 The Interpretability Hypothesis and the Feature Reassembly Hypothesis

Although some of the current generative theories and hypotheses on SLA do not make direct predictions on the role of pragmatic processes to the development of linguistic knowledge, it is important to air them for their direct implications in interpreting some of the findings reported in subsequent sections. On that note, different UG accounts to SLA claim dissimilar views of parameter resetting, depending on the capacity of interlanguage grammars to attain new values for interpretable and uninterpretable features. One such account is the *Interpretability Hypothesis* (IH) (Hawkins and Hattori, 2006; Tsimpli and Dimitrakopoulou, 2007). Proponents of the IH[2] claim that L2 uninterpretable features, which are purely syntactic in nature, are no longer available to adult learners, if they were not instantiated in the L1; this hypothesis is tied to assumptions related to the critical period hypothesis and the effects of this period limiting the potential to fully acquire languages after early childhood. That is, only features instantiated within the L1 and new interpretable features remain available. Uninterpretable features, in contrast, are argued to no longer

---

[2] The IH is actually a logical continuation of the Representational Deficit Hypothesis (Hawkins and Chan, 1997; Hawkins and Franceschina, 2004).

be available to adults due to critical period constraints, despite access to L2 input/lexicon that clearly exemplifies L2 features. This explains an adult inability to reset parameters, at least when they are contingent on the acquisition of new uninterpretable features.

Thus, the IH asserts that the underlying syntax of L2 grammars is destined to remain like the L1 grammar with localised (or surface) adjustments. In other words, L1 and L2 grammars are hypothesised to be inevitably distinct, on a continuum that is determined by the extent to which the L1/L2-particular grammars have unique feature compositions. Nevertheless, it is assumed that adult L2 learners can, and do, redeploy L1 features to be mapped onto newly acquired L2 morpho-phonological forms and acquire surface rules by way of *domain-general learning* (i.e., applying general learning strategies that can be used for learning in any area, in contrast to what is proposed in a modular view of the language faculty and of language acquisition). The IH would contend that the aforementioned assumptions explain seeming L2 successes while maintaining that ubiquitous L2 variability endures – that is, a non-native speaker will always show a range of differences in their use of a language (pronunciation, certain grammatical structures and so on) in comparison with native speakers – precisely because underlying L2 representations are non-target-like.

On the other hand, Lardiere (2008, 2009) proposed a somewhat different approach to analysing the process of acquiring additional languages, known as the FRH. Lardiere maintains that acquiring an L2 grammar is not a question of whether features are still available for selection from a universal inventory. In contrast, this author proposes that successful L2 acquisition is determined by whether L2 speakers can effectively (re)assemble existing L1 features into new L2 configurations. Specifically, Lardiere (2008, p. 235) illustrates this point maintaining that '[. . .] acquiring an L2 grammar is not just a matter of learners determining whether features are still available for selection from a universal inventory and are, in fact, selected. In particular, we need to consider how they are assembled or bundled together into lexical items (or functional categories), and then we must further consider the particular language-specific conditions under which they are phonologically realized'.

Thus, for the FRH, the pertinent question is how features are assembled and mapped to lexical items taking into consideration particular language-specific conditions under which they are phonologically realised. Two languages can select the same formal features such that a native speaker of language A acquiring language B would not need to 'reset' the parameter in question. Nevertheless, how a particular feature is assembled and the conditions of its expression in each of the two languages may be quite different. The learning task would then consist of appropriately re-configuring or re-assembling formal and semantic bundles in the L2 lexicon and determining the specific conditions under which their properties may or may not be morphophonologically expressed. That is, in addition to acquiring new features, the adult learner must redeploy the morphological expression of individual features from the way they are employed in the native language.

For the FRH, convergence hinges on whether L1 features take the same morpholexical expressions in the L2 and whether learners can effectively reconfigure them when this is not the case. The FRH contrasts sharply with the Interpretability Hypothesis account in that it claims that adult learners have unabridged UG access, interpretable and uninterpretable features alike, and in that it does not predict intrinsic difficulties in the domain of uninterpretable syntactic features. Given this, not only are L2ers expected to be able to acquire new feature specifications for uninterpretable syntactic features, but also it is expected that their ability to acquire the corresponding native-like underlying representations cannot be permanently lost even though their exposure to the new language takes place after the critical period for language acquisition.

2.3 The Interface Hypothesis

Taking a slightly different approach to the one just described, there are several other approaches to analysing acquisition in relation to the interfaces. These are especially related to the line taken in the present Element.

Departing from the fact that grammar consists of the computational system or narrow syntax, the output of which feeds into the PF and the LF at the interfaces between these levels (Bos et al., 2004), studies in this area in the adult L2 acquisition research agenda have provided controversial results. Some studies have shown that structures involving the interfaces are more difficult to acquire and more vulnerable to fossilisation than structures involving only narrow syntax, but other studies have revealed that despite the difficulty that integrating interpretative input from more than one module entails, adult L2 learners are able to acquire structures involving the interfaces.

Research in L2 acquisition has proposed that structures involving the interfaces (e.g., syntax-pragmatics and syntax-semantics) are particularly 'vulnerable' to processes such as attrition, fossilisation and incomplete acquisition (Montrul, 2002, 2004; Serratrice et al., 2004; Sorace, 2004; Tsimpli et al., 2004; Bruhn de Garavito and Valenzuela, 2006).[3] For example, Sorace (2004) and Serratrice et al. (2004) made the claim that structures involving narrow syntax are, by and large,

---

[3] For our purposes, we take the view that only external interfaces (i.e., syntax-pragmatics) are vulnerable. On this note, recall that Slabakova (2006, 2008) also proposes that there is no vulnerability at the syntax-semantic interface in line with others (e.g., Tsimpli and Sorace, 2006).

easier to acquire and less *vulnerable* than the ones involving the interfaces. Vulnerability, in these studies, refers to the propensity to attrition or lack of consolidation of the language structure or feature acquired. This kind of vulnerability has been shown to exist in various acquisitional scenarios, that is, bilingual acquisition, adult L2 acquisition and language loss or attrition. For example, in contexts of language attrition (loss), Sorace has put forward the idea that 'aspects of the grammar at the syntax-information structure interface are more vulnerable to attrition than purely syntactic ones' (Sorace, 2004, p. 143). That is, while formal syntactic mechanisms are resistant to attrition, so they tend to be acquired permanently, interfaces are more probable candidates for attrition because they are more complex than narrow syntax. For instance, the acquisition of some of the properties involved in the pro-drop parameter, that is, referential subject pronouns versus that-trace filter violations are interface properties, and thus, they are inherently more difficult to acquire (Sorace, 2011, 2012).

One way of explaining this kind of vulnerability to attrition is by suggesting that at the syntax-discourse level, the learner may hear apparently interchangeable sentences in the input, but with subtle contextual differences. Thus, the input for discourse-related properties is perhaps 'weaker', resulting in the delay of acquisition – these properties take longer to acquire – or permanent optionality – the learner continues to lack a solid ability to use the properties. L2 learners may also have processing difficulties in integrating different types of information pertaining to different domains. All this may yield the construction of interlanguage grammars, that is, the grammatical systems that the non-native speaker relies on, as long as their acquisition process has not yet led them to having a command equal to that of a native speaker that may differ in interface areas from native grammars in significant ways.

Most studies, however, have focused on the acquisition of a relatively narrow set of structures, for example, overt versus null pronominal subjects, word order and object expression, in different language acquisition scenarios by different populations in a quite wide range of languages. The acquisition of overt versus null pronominal subjects relates to the Pro-drop Parameter involving the syntax-information structure interface. In pro-drop languages, such as Greek, Italian and Spanish, overt subjects are strongly favoured when they introduce new information, when a contrast is established or a focus is required. On the contrary, null subjects are preferred when there is no switch in reference in a series of sentences in discourse, and when there is no need for focus and contrast. Serratrice et al. (2004) investigated the acquisition of overt versus null pronominal subjects in an Italian/English bilingual child compared to two groups of monolingual children whose language development was at a similar stage (measured by the average number of words that they produced in each utterance). This study showed that in Italian the bilingual child produced overt pronominal subjects in contexts where monolingual, prefer a null subject. In addition, the bilingual child used post-verbal strong object pronouns rather than preverbal weak pronominal clitics. Similar results were obtained in adult L2 acquisition. Adult L2 learners of null subject languages whose first language (L1) does not allow null subjects apparently use null subjects correctly in obligatory contexts but overuse overt subjects in contexts requiring a null pronoun (Sorace and Filiaci, 2006) in the L2. These results indicate cross-linguistic influence in specific contexts at the syntax-pragmatics interface.

Similar findings were reported by Lozano (2006a, 2006b) who investigated features related to the lexicon-syntax interface and the syntax-information structure interface (e.g., focus) in Greek learners of Spanish at the upper intermediate, lower advanced and upper advanced proficiency levels, and native controls. Participants had to judge Subject–Verb and Verb–Subject word orders with intransitive verbs (unergative – intransitive verbs that are used with agentive subjects, like *resign*, and unaccusative verbs – those whose subject is not the agent, but the experiencer, such as *fall*) in a Contextualised Acceptability judgement task. This phenomenon involves the lexicon-syntax interface (Unaccusative Hypothesis) and the syntax-information structure interface (focus). The results showed that although learners of Spanish showed knowledge of word order at the lexicon-syntax interface, they presented persistent deficits with the discourse interpretive features, and hence the realisation of focus at the syntactical level. However, it is not clear whether such knowledge is provided by UG or by their L1 grammar since Greek and Spanish are very similar in this respect.

In contrast to those studies, other studies have revealed that native-like grammars can be attained, even in areas that rely heavily on context for interpretation and involve the interfaces (Dekydtspotter et al., 1999/2000; Dekydtspotter and Sprouse, 2001; Borgonovo et al., 2005, 2006; Borgonovo et al., 2006). For example, Borgonovo et al. (2005, 2006) investigated the acquisition of verbal mood (the distinction between indicative and subjunctive) in Spanish relative clauses by adult English learners of Spanish at the intermediate and advanced proficiency levels compared to a group of native speakers of Spanish, using a Grammaticality Judgement and a Truth-Value Judgement task. In Spanish, the choice of mood in such contexts depends on the specificity status of the modified DP, but not on grammaticality. That is, the presence of indicative correlates with the specificity of the DP (3a), whereas subjunctive is needed when the head is non-specific (3b):

(3)   a. Compré una mesa donde **caben** 6 personas.
             'I bought a table where 6 people **fit (IND)**'.
         b. Tiene que encontrar una mesa donde **quepan** 6 personas.
             'S/he has to find a table where 6 people **fit (SUBJ)**'.

Although in English mood does not signal specificity, L1 English learners of
Spanish were shown to acquire target distinctions (the contrast between the
indicative versus subjunctive in a variety of contexts) without any explicit
teaching of this phenomenon. However, there were clear differences related to
participants' proficiency levels: advanced learners behaved like natives, but that
was not the case with intermediate learners. Dialectal variation amongst the
native speakers was also found to have effects on the acquisition of this interface
phenomenon.

In a different study, Borgonovo et al. (2006) investigated syntactic correlates
of the semantic notion of specificity by looking at the acquisition of object drop
and topicalisation by Brazilian Portuguese (BP) learners of Spanish as an L2. In
Spanish, specific objects may not be dropped, and topicalised specific DPs
appear in the clitic left dislocation (CLLD) construction (Cinque, 1990). On
the other hand, non-specific objects may be dropped while non-specific topics
take the non-clitic left dislocation (non-CLLD) construction. These facts contrast in important ways with BP, in which object omission and non-CLLD are
not related to specificity in any direct way. The results from this study showed
that BP learners of Spanish were able to make the correct association between
the interpretation of specificity and its effects on syntax in spite of the fact that
specificity does not play the same role in their L1. This indicates that interfaces
may be inherently difficult, but acquisition of their properties is possible,
nonetheless.

To summarise, whereas one set of studies looking at the acquisition of
interface phenomena suggests that L2 acquisition of structures involving the
syntax-discourse interface are acquired late, and can cause difficulties even at
the very advanced stages of development, others seem to show that they are
acquirable. In order to reconcile these findings, it may be necessary to differentiate between different interfaces or between phenomena within each interface.
This is the emerging pattern in Tsimpli and Sorace (2006). Specifically, it is
necessary to distinguish between syntax-discourse and syntax-semantics interfaces: the former involves a 'higher' level of integration with properties outside
the grammar proper (see however Belletti, 2004 for a different view), whereas
the latter comprises the interaction of syntax with interpretable features internal
to the language system.

The other difference is that phenomena at the syntax-discourse interface
typically involve preferences and uses that are appropriate as opposed to others

that are not, whereas syntax-semantics properties typically entail distinctions between what is, or is not, grammatical (e.g., Focus in Greek, which is the specific property investigated by Tsimpli and Sorace, 2006). To that end, Sorace and Filiaci (2006) report on an experimental study with 14 English near-native speakers of Italian. The study applied a picture verification task, which showed that the learners' preferences for interpretations of overt subject pronouns as co-referential with a topic antecedent were significantly higher than those of 20 monolingual natives. The two groups, however, were indistinguishable with respect to the interpretation of null subject pronouns. The study explores a processing explanation for this pattern and suggests (on the basis of Carminati's, 2002, 2005 results) that near-natives may make more extended use of an option that is also used by native speakers, but more sparingly.

In the light of these findings, we can see how it is important to investigate different interface phenomena with a precise analysis of what is entailed by the various interface properties. However, the Interface Hypothesis developed by Sorace and her colleagues does not contain details on the nature of pragmatic processes and on how the relationship between language, world knowledge and general cognition operates. Theoretical perspectives such as the ones provided by the RT propose specific insights on those issues and, therefore, offer potential for explaining different kinds of processing challenges in first and second languages, depending on the kinds of tasks used in experimental research.

2.4 Procedural Meaning Across Languages

The distinction between conceptual and procedural meaning, established within the framework of RT (see Section 1), has been developed in various (and not always compatible) directions by different linguists. Some developments take a general, essentially theoretical view, while others rely on actual data and focus on how cross-linguistic variation in procedural expressions may be approached. In this section, only the developments of taking a cross-linguistic approach will be considered.

One of the generally accepted characteristics of procedural meaning is that it is language-specific and difficult to translate (Wilson, 2011, 2016). And yet, a clear intuition is that cross-linguistically comparable items (such as pronouns, mood, tenses, prosody or discourse connectives) do not encode very different procedures in separate languages. Hence, how is the cross-linguistic architecture of procedural meaning to be conceived? Where are those commonalities and differences located?

In cross-linguistic studies on procedural meaning, three types of expressions have often been considered, namely tenses and (to a lesser extent) pronouns and discourse connectives. European – especially Romance languages and English – have been the main object of comparison. Therefore, our main concern in the following paragraphs will be with these kinds of expressions, and especially tenses in English and Romance languages. They hold special interest in relation to deepening knowledge of how grammar and pragmatics interact in SLA processes. Discourse markers are another topic that has offered insights into SLA at the interfaces, so some research on these will be brought up in Section 2.4.3.

The way in which categories are realised varies in typologically dissimilar languages. In Germanic and Romance languages, lexical categories (nouns, adjectives, verbs and adverbs) tend to occur in independent items, while functional categories may appear as independent items (as in pronouns, conjunctions connectives) or as bound morphemes (as case, person, mood, tense and aspect exponents). Thus, conceptual and procedural meaning may coexist within a single linguistic item. This has been accounted for in two contrasting ways.

On the one hand, it has been alleged (Wilson, 2011, 2016; Moeschler et al., 2012; Grisot, 2015, 2018; Grisot and Moeschler, 2014; Moeschler, 2016, 2012; Wharton, 2016) that the distinction between conceptual and procedural meaning is gradual, so that single expressions may be at the same time conceptual and procedural in different proportions: for example all causal connectives involve the concept CAUSE and all tenses involve the concept TIME (which is further specificised as PAST, PRESENT or FUTURE). Contrastingly, a strict separation of conceptual and procedural meaning has been advocated by other scholars (Escandell-Vidal and Leonetti, 2002, 2011; Saussure, 2011; Amenós-Pons, 2010, 2011, 2023; Escandell-Vidal, 2016, 2019a and b). Those adopting this view have argued that linguistic categories are sets of features (not complete lexical items) and individual features cannot be conceptual and procedural at the same time, even if words may constitute bundles of conceptual and procedural features (Escandell-Vidal, 2016).

Escandell-Vidal (2016) claims that a functional category targeting the inferential system (e.g., pronouns) may include procedural instructions and conceptual representations; in such cases, the conceptual information is dependent on the procedure. The encoded procedure 'takes the conceptual content as a parameter', adding specific conditions (Saussure, 2011, p. 65). For example, the procedure encoded in English by the pronoun *she* is a processing instruction (a computational operation to locate an entity) and two specific restrictions (the entity must be both accessible and female). Only one of those restrictions (the fact that the referred entity must be a female) involves a concept, which is not accessed independently of the procedure, but as a requirement to restrict the referential space.

In each theoretical model, the overall view on how conceptual and procedural meaning relate to each other has direct consequences on how empirical data are interpreted. This will be shown in the following pages, by contrasting two alternative cross-linguistic descriptions of tenses, based on competing assumptions.

2.4.1 The Mixed Conceptual and Procedural Meaning Approach

The approach that considers conceptual and procedural meaning to be amenable to combination in a single linguistic unit (Moeschler, 2012; Moeschler et al., 2012; Grisot and Moeschler, 2014; Moeschler, 2015, Grisot, 2018) postulates that tenses have robust semantics, inspired by different combinations of the Reichenbachian coordinates E (the event), S (the point of Speech) and R (a point for reference). This semantics tends to be cross-linguistically stable within genealogically related languages. In this model, the Reichenbachian coordinates are seen as conceptual, because they include the concept TIME. Each tense systematically incorporates a specific combination of the coordinates, which act as a template of variables that must be contextually saturated.

Additionally, tenses integrate a set of more flexible features, defined as follows:

- [± narrative]. This feature refers to the temporal ordering of events within a sequence. The [+ narrative] feature indicates that a chronological order may be inferred, while a [-narrative] feature implies that chronological relations are not relevant.
- [± subjective]. This feature relates to the presence or absence of a point of view, which may in turn be implicit or explicit. A feature value [+ subjective] indicates that the utterance where the tense is found incorporate a subject of consciousness, that is, a specific perspectival viewpoint on the situation depicted. A negative value on that feature implies that such viewpoint is not available.
- [implicit] / [explicit]. This feature is subordinated to the [+ subjective] feature and refers to the fact that the attribution of the perspectival viewpoint to someone is explicit or implicit. If a tense contextual value is [− subjective], the implicit / explicit distinction does not operate.

The latter set of features is viewed as procedural: these features are abstract, largely unconscious and difficult to verbalise; they act as constraints on the inferential processing. The approach taken by Moeschler and colleagues is not related to generative grammar, so the authors do not consider whether or not these features are part of a universal repository of UG features.

Grisot (2018) argues that the main tenets of the mixed conceptual and procedural meaning model are empirically validated by the fact that competent speakers can easily ascertain, with very little interindividual variation, if an utterance is located in the past, present or future (which are conceptual notions). On the other hand, there is frequent disagreement in the estimations of temporal ordering and viewpoint effect within a sentence (a fact that Grisot sees as the consequence of the procedural nature of viewpoint aspect and temporal ordering features).

Crucially, this model assumes that the values of the procedural features are not inherent to specific tenses. On the contrary, every tense within a language may potentially develop different value combinations, which are as follows (see Figure 1).

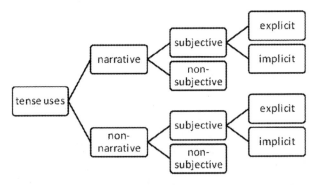

Figure 1 Types of tense uses (Moeschler, 2016, p. 130).

Examples of diverse feature combinations in the uses of the French past tenses are given below:

(4)   Hier, je suis allé chez le coiffeur. Il *m'a teint* les cheveux en roux.
        'Yesterday I went [Compound Past] to the barber. He *dyed* **(CP)** my hair red'
        Compound past: [+ narrative], [+ subjective], [explicit]

(5)   Mare sauta dans le train. Dix minutes plus tard, le train *déraillait*.
        'Mary jumped [Simple Past] on the train. Ten minutes later, the train *derailed* **[Imperfect]**.'
        Imperfect: [+ narrative], [+ subjective], [implicit]

(6)   Paul entra dans un café. Il *commanda* une bière.
        'Paul went [Simple Past] into a café. He *ordered* **(SP)** a beer'.
        Simple past: [+ narrative], [− subjective]

(7)   Qu'elle était stupide! *Pensa-t-elle*.
        'How stupid she was [Imperfect]! She *thought* **(SP)**'
        Simple past: [− narrative], [+ subjective], [explicit]

(8)   En 1805, Napoléon *se déclarait* empereur.
        'In 1805, Napoleon *declared himself* (IMP) emperor'.
        Imperfect: [− narrative], [+ subjective], [implicit]

In utterance (4), the chronology of the events may be inferred, and the subjective perspective is made explicit by the first-person pronouns. In (5), the chronology is made explicit by the expression *ten minutes later*. Mary's subjective viewpoint may be inferred, but it is not explicitly expressed in the sentence containing the imperfect tense; in (6), the chronological order of the events may be inferred, but no subjective viewpoint is available; in (7), the free indirect style allows the representation of a previous utterance or a thought, explicitly attributed to a character by means of the pronoun *she*; finally, in (8), the imperfect tense is located in a non-narrative environment; a subjective perspective is found, but not explicitly attributed (Napoléon is the subject of the verb, but not necessarily the subject of consciousness).

For every tense, all feature combinations are theoretically possible, but not actually found, nor equally exploited in the corresponding tenses of different languages. This is a crucial point, since the cross-linguistic variation in the use of the comparable tenses found in different languages relates to the distinct feature combinations that are frequent, available or impossible in each language.

So far, the mixed conceptual and procedural approach to tenses has not been directly applied to L2 acquisition research. Nevertheless, Grisot (2018) implemented a modelisation of this approach in the fields of Natural Language Processing and Machine Translation. Statistical machine translation systems were trained on automatically tagged data, with the features provided by the model of temporal reference developed. According to the researchers, this gave better results in tense translation than did other systems which do not make use of those features. As a result, Grisot (2018) stresses the need to develop linguistic and pragmatic models of language that are empirically and experimentally derived for their validation by successful implementation in applied fields, such as natural language processing, machine translation and second language teaching.

2.4.2 The Full Procedural Meaning Approach

This approach (Escandell-Vidal and Leonetti, 2002, 2011; Amenós-Pons, 2010, 2011, 2023; Saussure, 2011; Escandell-Vidal, 2016, 2019a and b) argues that the conceptual / procedural distinction is linked to the contrast between lexical and functional categories. Lexical categories encode phonological, conceptual and computational attributes, whereas functional categories do not map onto conceptual representations, but rather encode only phonological and computational information. The computational attributes of lexical categories are only relevant to syntactic computations, while those of functional categories are operational; they 'consist of directions, functions or rules specifying the way in which other constituents are to be processed and fit together in composition' (Escandell-Vidal, 2016, p. 82). Thus, the latter type of computational attributes consists of abstract, procedural information to be read by the conceptual-intentional systems. Procedural meaning can thus be equated to the interpretable features of functional categories, as described by Chomsky (1995) (Escandell-Vidal and Leonetti, 2002, 2011).

This point of departure establishes a crucial difference between this approach and the one described in the previous section. In Moeschler and Grisot's view, the procedural features of the tenses have an ambiguous nature, between semantics and pragmatics; the potential values (positive and negative) of procedural features are linguistically encoded, but their materialisation is dependent on specific discourse requirements. Contrastingly, in the full procedural meaning approach, procedural meaning fully belongs to the semantics of a language. According to Escandell-Vidal and Leonetti (2011), procedural meaning is both rigid and schematic. That is, features encoded by inflectional morphology are invariable and underlie all the different uses and interpretations that can be identified. Yet these features are *schematic* in the sense that they underdetermine the potential interpretations the expression can lead to. A procedural expression (whose meaning is fixed and unique) can give rise to a wide range of interpretations, depending on the discourse environment and according to the mental representations activated when building the context in which we process the utterance where the expression is used. In contrast, conceptual meanings are much more flexible and adaptable, depending on specific interpretive needs.

Escandell-Vidal (2016) argues that the processing instructions encoded in interpretable features can operate on different levels of representation: they may contribute to establishing the propositional representation expressed by an utterance (this is the case of aspectual markers and information structure markers). But they may also contribute to identifying implicated premises, conclusions, illocutionary intentions and propositional attitudes (this is what discourse markers and illocutionary indicators do). Within this approach, Escandell-Vidal (2021) and Amenós-Pons (2023) have developed cross-linguistic descriptions of the Romance future tense and of the Romance compound and simple past tenses, respectively. In the following paragraphs, we provide an outline of Escandell's analysis of the Romance future tense, as an example of this approach.

In modern Romance languages (except for Romanian and some Italian vernaculars), a synthetic, inflectional future form exists, having developed from a periphrastic source: the Latin obligative construction 'Infinitive + habere'. In most of these Romance languages, this future tense may receive not only interpretations related to chronology, but also conjectural interpretations. Examples of both interpretations in Spanish are given below.

(9)   (Echador de cartas) Te casarás y tendrás muchos hijos.
        '(Fortune teller) You'll marry (FUT) and you'll have (FUT) lots of children'.

(10)   No ha telefoneado. *Estará* ocupado.
        'He has not phoned. He must be (FUT) busy'.

However, the restrictions that apply to conjectural readings (like the one shown in (10)) differ across the Romance languages. In Spanish, Italian and Portuguese, conjectural interpretations correspond to a very high percentage of the future tense usage (Escandell-Vidal, 2010, 2014), while in French, and also in Catalan, the mere existence of these interpretations in present-day spontaneous production is a debated issue (Aramón i Serra, 1957; Le Querler, 1990; Tasmowski and Dendale, 1998; Rocci, 2000; Pérez Saldanya, 2008; De Saussure and Morency, 2012).

Escandell-Vidal (2021) describes the semantics of the simple future in terms of features; the core features of that tense are common to all Romance varieties, but other features differ. Thus, the core meaning of the Romance future encodes an instruction [for the hearer] to build the eventuality described by the sentence radical (the proposition *p*), as the representation of a situation (event situation, abbreviated as ES) that cannot be accessed from an information acquisition situation (information situation, or IS), in which the discourse situation (DS) is included. The core semantic features do not specifically relate to time, nor to conjecture, but to the information source: the situation described is (at the IS) only available as an inference of the speaker. This implies that the future tense has an inherent evidential meaning.

Despite the existence of common Romance features, the ultimate materialisations of the simple future in the different languages will vary depending on the values that other cross-linguistically shared features have taken in each of them. These features and their variation are represented below in Table 2.

Thus, following Escandell-Vidal's proposal, the Romance future is always non-factual. In all the Romance languages except Catalan it is also [+ deictic]; this means that (in these languages) the IS is related to the speaker's perceptual field. The Catalan future is the only one among the Romance language future tenses that is independent from the IS; as a result, this language disallows conjectural readings, as opposed to French, Italian, Spanish and Portuguese. However, the French simple future imposes a [+ Forward] relation between IS and ES: thus, all eventualities, in French, call for a future verification. This is not

Table 2 The semantics of the simple future tense in Romance
(Escandell-Vidal, 2021, p. 23).

CORE MEANING	IS | ES DS ⊂ IS				
PARAMETERS	CATALAN	FRENCH	ITALIAN	SPANISH	PORTUGUESE
ES [± Factual]	–	–	–	–	–
IS[± Deictic]	–	+	+	+	+
IS | ES [± Forward]	+	+	–	–	–

required in Italian, Spanish and Portuguese and, as a result, conjectural uses of the future tense may be more pervasive. In this account (unlike in the mixed conceptual and procedural approach), the ± feature values are stable and are not subject to contextual variation within a single language.

A general consequence of this approach to procedural and conceptual meaning is that a whole family of multifarious grammatical phenomena can be explained as the result of the interplay between various types of linguistic meaning and conceptual representations. The prediction is that any possible mismatch between conceptual and procedural elements will always be resolved by obeying the constraints imposed by procedural ones (Escandell-Vidal and Leonetti, 2011; Escandell-Vidal, 2016). This has been analysed in aspectual clashes, coercion phenomena with copulas, non-temporal uses of verb tenses and evidential interpretations of tensed sentences. For instance, in the tense and aspect domain, many interpretative effects have been described for the Romance imperfect tense when it is used with a telic predicate (De Saussure, 2003, 2013; Leonetti and Escandell-Vidal, 2003; Amenós-Pons, 2010, 2015). An example is given in the contrast between (11) and (12) below.

(11)   Ayer, el avión **despegaba** a las siete.
         'Yesterday, the plane **was taking off (IMP)** at seven o'clock'.

(12)   Ayer, el avión **despegó** a las siete.
         'Yesterday, the plane **took off (SP)** at seven o'clock'.

The imperfect tense incorporates the aspectual feature [-perfective], while the simple perfect contains the feature [+ perfective]. Given their procedural nature, these interpretable features are rigid and restrict the mental representation that the listener builds of the lexical elements (the telic predicate *take off*). Thus, when the imperfect is used with a telic predicate like *despegar* 'take off', the event is interpreted contextually as atelic, that is, it is represented as unbounded. Since the utterance incorporates a temporal adverb, the simplest way (i.e., the one that requires less processing effort) to harmonise the explicit information provided is to construct a prospective interpretation of the event by means of aspectual coercion (Moens and Steedman 1988). On the other hand, coercion effect does not occur in the simple past, which promotes a factual interpretation of the telic predicate.

In (11) the imperfectivity of the tense conflicts with the telicity of the predicate. Solving this mismatch requires a cognitive effort, which is compensated by obtaining an interpretive effect: the event is seen from a specific perspective, which does not correspond to that of the speaker at the time of issuing the statement, but to that of someone (the same speaker or another person) at an earlier time (De Saussure, 2003, 2013). None of this occurs in (12), where the perfectivity of the verb tense fits well with the boundedness of the telic predicate. Thus, in (11) the semantic mismatch resolution gives rise to a characteristic interpretive effect. This is linked to an additional processing effort, which some generative approaches consider characteristic of the operations that take place at the interfaces (Jackendoff, 2002).

In the theoretical domain, this approach has led to a set of powerful generalisations related to the main principles of reinterpretation processes and to the consequences that can be derived from these processes for linguistic theory and for the grammar/pragmatics interface (Escandell-Vidal and Leonetti, 2011, 2012). In the applied domain, it has led to specific hypotheses on some processing challenges for L2 acquisition. For native speakers, access to the meaning of procedural expressions is automatic and largely unconscious: these expressions constitute a kind of skeleton of the language, providing support to conceptual representations (Sperber, 1996). Contrastingly, apprehending the meaning of procedural expressions in an L2 is particularly difficult due to the abstract nature of this kind of meaning (Escandell-Vidal, 2006). Furthermore, the uses of a procedural expression whose interpretation requires a greater degree of pragmatic enrichment (as in the case of the use of the imperfect tense seen in utterance (11) above) will be particularly challenging. This is due to the cognitive cost involved in relating linguistic meaning and contextual assumptions in a consistent way. Thus, the challenge of learning an L2 grammar does not come only from the grammar itself, but also from the cognitive operations required by the interpretation of linguistic forms in the various discourse environments in which they appear.

2.4.3 Experimental Studies on Procedural Semantics: Discourse Markers in L2s

The original conception of procedural meaning was developed in the analysis by Diane Blakemore (1987) of discourse markers: particles whose meaning is only describable in terms of a kind of instruction on how the proposition or phrase that they introduce should be understood in relation to other information in the discourse. Since then, a wide range of empirical studies have sought evidence of how we process procedural expressions.

Several researchers have pointed out that discourse particles pose a challenge for L2 learners (see Zufferey, 2015; Loureda et al., 2021 and references therein). The complexity is partly due to their procedural nature, which prevents their meaning from being accessible to introspection. Moreover, from the point of view of language contrast, the functional correspondences among discourse particles are complex, making it difficult to find direct equivalents between two languages. Even apparently analogous markers in two different languages are almost always subject to different usage restrictions in each of them.

Learning discourse particles in an L2 may also be hampered by two types of 'extra' processing effort (Loureda et al., 2021, p. 197). On the one hand, *quantitative overexertion*, due to the lack of automatisation of the procedural meaning of the L2 expressions; on the other hand, *qualitative overexertion*, since the difficulty of accessing the procedural meaning of the discourse markers increases the processing cost of discourse information as a whole.

Empirical studies have implemented eye-tracking technology to investigate how discourse markers in different languages affect the interpretation of utterances. These studies focus on understanding written texts, as the technology that eye-trackers offer provides a window into how we process language during reading, measuring the time and the ways that our eyes move as we read a text or sentence (Loureda et al., 2021). Depending on how quickly or slowly a participant moves their eyes as they read, as well as whether and how much they may stop reading to look back at a previous stretch of writing, these experiments provide evidence on the processing mechanisms that are used and the amount of processing effort needed for the words and expressions analysed (Canestrelli and Mak y Sanders, 2013).

For instance, studies on the effect of causal connectives like 'therefore' or 'however' (Spanish 'por tanto' or 'sin embargo') and similar expressions in other languages have been carried out. Recio Fernández (2020) compared the processing of argumentative relations marked and unmarked by discourse particles by speakers of Spanish as L1, by learners of Spanish as L2 at advanced level (C1 of the CEFR) and by learners at lower intermediate level (B1 of the CEFR). She found that, in speakers of lower L2 proficiency (level B1), the presence of the discourse particle *por tanto* 'therefore' produces maximum effects: firstly, it facilitates the processing of the utterance where the discourse marker is used, compared to the same utterances presented without the marker. And in addition, the presence of the discourse marker facilitates the processing of the sequence as a whole. But the use of this marker had no discernible effect on C1 learners, whose strategic competence enabled them to infer the appropriate discourse relations without the help of the marker.

Recio Fernández (2020) also studied how the presence of the Spanish discourse markers *por tanto* 'therefore' and *sin embargo* 'although' affects the resolution of interpretative conflicts in utterances that include unexpected cause and consequence relations. In native speakers of Spanish, and in non-native learners at C1 level, an increase in processing effort when resolving the unexpected relations was experimentally observed. On the other hand, in learners at B1 level, the behaviour detected was somewhat different, depending on the type of argumentative relation. In causal relations (marked with *therefore*), the developmental stage of these learners' L2 strategic competence enables them to attempt to infer ways to repair the interpretative conflict. In contrast, in counter-argumentative relations (marked with *although*), the unexpected cause and consequence relations lead the learners to give up on inferring how to repair the conflict instead of attempting repair. In sum, C1 learners need more time than native speakers to process utterances, but the procedures employed are similar. This is not the case with B1 learners, who exhibit partly different behaviour when resolving interpretative conflicts.

2.5 RT and SLA at the Interfaces

In this section, we summarise a set of studies on L2 acquisition that have used the analytic tools provided by RT to inquire into different syntax-semantics-pragmatics interface phenomena.

Liszka (2004) shows that analysing along relevance-theoretic lines some aspects of grammatical deficits in the L2 production of learners belonging to a specific native language background can explain the nature of the obstacles they face. Focusing on how German, Japanese and Chinese EFL learners recover explicatures while processing English utterances of sentences that include different verb tense uses, Liszka (2004) identifies and explains some obstacles that non-native speakers face and pragmalinguistic strategies that these L2 learners resort to in searching for optimal relevance. She argues that, if a certain linguistic feature is not available at logical form, a learner might nevertheless access non-linguistic resources, such as encyclopaedic representations, and retrieve an approximation of the form required in the construction of an utterance aiming for optimal relevance. However, successful utterance interpretation and use would be more probabilistic than for native speakers who have the relevant feature specified in their grammars. This clearly suggests that pragmatic representations, as such, do not exist independently from utterances; unlike syntactic features, pragmatic representations are formed and accessed online; they do not come from any kind of universal repository of features. Liszka's research successfully demonstrates how the relevance-theoretic approach makes it possible to predict and elucidate L2 acquisition problems with regard to the acquisition of tense and aspect, but it also shows some ways in which L2 acquisition processes offer evidence in favour of relevance-theoretic assumptions.

Ahern, Amenós-Pons and Guijarro-Fuentes carried out a series of studies (Ahern et al., 2014, 2016, 2017a and b, 2020, 2023a; Amenós-Pons et al., 2019) on the development of the ability of L2 Spanish learners to interpret metarepresentational, evidentiality-related uses of the imperfect tense, the indicative/ subjunctive mood alternation and the contrast between chronological and conjectural interpretations of the future tense. The studies examined these tense and mood uses as a means to explore acquisition of grammatical combinations requiring integration with pragmatic inferential processes.

Ahern et al. (2014, 2016) reported on a study on the interpretation of Spanish utterances with indicative/subjunctive alternation in concessive (clauses introduced by *aunque* 'although') and conditional (introduced by *si* 'if') constructions. The research was developed by applying a questionnaire (thirty multiple-choice items to groups of L1 French and L1 English learners of L2 Spanish at CEFR levels B2 and C1, in a non-immersion institutional context. The learners responded to questions about the interpretations of utterances (including tense and mood uses with assertive, non-assertive, quotative or *irrealis* readings) that required the identification of grammar-embedded cues. Overall, the L2 learners at advanced levels experienced much more difficulty than L1 native speakers. The variability observed across the item results suggests that the presence of explicit situational, non-grammatical cues facilitates comprehension of the utterance; conversely, interpreting combinations of non-prototypical associations of linguistic features significantly increased difficulty.

Despite considerable individual variation, several general regularities were shown: (1) Neither the L1 nor the level of proficiency were observed to affect ability for successful use of the L2 procedural expressions that we had studied. (2) L2 learners tend to rely on explicit conceptual cues. (3) Incomplete acquisition of procedural units: the grammatical units which are procedural in L1 seem to be processed in L2 as incomplete conceptual approximations. They are used less efficiently and require more time to be activated. (4) Procedural units do not form a homogeneous block from the perspective of L2 acquisition. Factors such as frequency of use, amount of explicit contextual cues and online resolution of interpretative conflicts all affect learnability of these units.

Amenós-Pons et al. (2017, 2018, 2019) studied how L1 French learners of L2 Spanish at four different levels of proficiency (A2, B1, B2 and C1, according to the CEFR) dealt with potentially difficult uses of Spanish past tenses, as detected in previous studies (Amenós-Pons, 2010, 2015). Their answers were compared to those of a control group of European Spanish speakers. This was done by means of a multiple-choice task, containing six items per condition (progressive and quotative imperfect), combined with distractors (different past and present tense forms.

The study included (among other uses) two different interpretations of the imperfect indicative (IMP) tense, namely progressive and quotative, as illustrated below in utterances (19) and (20).

(19)   Juan **preparaba** la cena en la cocina, pero tuvo que salir urgentemente y no pudo terminar.
        'Juan **was making (IMP)** dinner in the kitchen, but he had to go out suddenly and didn't manage to finish making it'. (progressive interpretation)

(20)   Ya telefoneé a Ernesto. **Terminaba** un capítulo, **compraba** unas cervezas y **venía** para acá.
        'I phoned (SP) Ernesto. He **was finishing (IMP)** a chapter, **getting (IMP)** some beer and **coming round (IMP)**'. (quotative interpretation)

The semantics of imperfect tense is generally assumed to be similar in Spanish and French. Progressive interpretations are frequent in both languages. However, quotative interpretations are less common in French than in Spanish; in many cases, when expressing prospectivity or hearsay, the construction *être* (in imperfect) + *gerund* is preferred in French (unlike in Spanish), rather than the simple imperfect form. Still, metarepresentational, quotative-like interpretations of imperfect are occasionally found in French.

The hypothesis put forward about the results is that quotative utterances are difficult for French-speaking learners of Spanish to interpret not only because their availability is limited in French and the environments in which they are found do not fully coincide in the two languages, but also because they require accessing contextually determined assumptions, which requires considerable cognitive effort. This effort is the result of an inherently demanding task, namely, the processing of incongruent semantic features (imperfectivity and telicity) and resolving the semantic mismatch by accessing a context where the event in imperfect is understood as the representation of a previous thought or an utterance, rather than a fact or situation that took place in the past. It was concluded that, on one hand, the process of acquisition involves feature reassembly in SLA, even in closely related grammatical units and language pairings. On the other hand, solving interpretive conflicts arising at the grammar/pragmatics interface is also an issue that cannot be ignored.

Building on Escandell-Vidal's (2021) analysis of the Romance future tense, Ahern et al. (2020) investigated the cross-linguistic effects on the acquisition of non-chronological – specifically, conjectural and concessive – interpretations of the simple and compound future tenses (S-FUT and COMP-FUT) in L2 Spanish, as illustrated below:

(21)   Llaman a la puerta. **Será** Juan. (Conjectural interpretation)
         'They are knocking at the door. That's probably Juan' (S-FUT).

(22)   La puerta no ha sido forzada. El ladrón **habrá entrado** por la ventana.
         (Conjectural interpretation)
         'The door has not been forced. The burglar **must have entered (COMP-FUT)**
         through the window'.

(23)   **Será** muy listo, pero no lo parece. (Concessive interpretation)
         'He **may be (S-FUT)** very smart, but s/he doesn't seem like it'.

In particular, the study sought to compare the intricacies of the role of L1 transfer in L2 Spanish acquisition, by L1 French speakers, at two different proficiency levels of L2 Spanish (CEFR B2 and C1), yet with similar learning experiences. Results of two written grammatical acceptability judgement tasks showed clear language transfer effects. The results also indicated that the learner groups took advantage of sensitivity to the role of lexical aspect in judging the appropriate interpretations of future tense, suggestive of cognitive processes at the discourse-syntax interface that are activated independently from any effects of conscious learning or instruction.

Thus, it was concluded that, when acquiring the uses of the future tense in L2 Spanish, L2 learners tend to operate within the limits of the interpretative strategies and routines of their own native language. Still, getting acquainted with an L2 form does not automatically entail acquiring all its semantic features and its discourse potentialities. Mapping L2 forms onto meaning is a complex and lengthy task that needs to be distinguished from merely learning the form, even in the deceptively simple case of the Romance future tense.

On the other hand, a study on bilingual speakers' representations of future tense uses, Ahern et al. (2023c) focused on Majorcan Catalan–Spanish bilinguals' use of this tense for expressing conjectural evidential meaning in their two L1s. Conjectural interpretations of the future tense are rare in Catalan, while in Spanish they are more frequent than chronological ones. A group of 97 bilingual speakers, with varying language dominance measures, performed two tasks in both languages: firstly, choosing between the future tense and two other ways of expressing conjecture; and secondly, judging the acceptability of conjectural uses of the future. The bilinguals' responses were compared to those of a group of thirty-six monolingual European Spanish speakers. The results indicate that bilinguals use the future tense to express conjecture less often than monolinguals, both in Catalan and in Spanish. However, all the groups showed awareness of the aspectual restrictions on the future tense as an expression of conjecture. The sensitivity of bilingual speakers to the factors that make conjectural uses of the tense appropriate could not be correlated with language dominance. In was concluded, in reference to Lardiere's (2009) FRH, that these bilinguals did not show evidence of reassembling features. They maintain the features of the Catalan future tense in Spanish, and simply use this tense in a more restricted way than Peninsular Spanish monolinguals. Thus, the study provided empirical evidence showing how the grammatical means by which bilinguals express conjecture vary, in contrast to those of monolinguals, stemming from the contact and interaction that takes place between languages with slightly differentiated restrictions.

All these studies suggest that the basic tenets of RT, as well as its applications to the study of linguistic meaning, tie in well with the approach to L2 acquisition phenomena along some of the fundamental Interface-Hypothesis related lines of enquiry. Interface approaches to SLA focus on the relationship of the faculty of language and other cognitive modules. However, in the SLA literature the details of such relationship are generally left unspecified; that is, the discourse/ pragmatic conditions affecting the different kinds of expressions studied in such research are often mentioned without any commitment to a framework in which their functioning can be described. In contrast, the interactions between linguistic structures and pragmatic interpretation processes have been at the center of attention of many RT scholars; the description of such interactions may be one of the crucial contributions of RT to the study of SLA at the interfaces.

Relating generative SLA hypotheses to RT insights are useful to integrate specific empirical results into a self-contained, coherent vision of verbal communication, where the role of linguistic expressions and the role of pragmatic information are integrated in precise way. The key to such integration lies in the notion of context, understood not as a set of external, objective variables, but as an array of mental representations actively selected online by the hearer, guided by expectations of relevance.

Thus, key RT concepts might be incorporated into current SLA models and implemented in investigating dynamic, non-linear and – at times – erratic L2 growth. The fundamental resemblances between RT and SLA theories thinking could be capitalised on at a more general level and at a more practical level; in particular, the capacities that language users possess constitute theoretically useful concepts to be incorporated into theoretical and empirical investigations. Therefore, SLA researchers need to pay attention to multiple sources of linguistic information that conjointly interact in the course of ensuring language development.

3 What Are the Key Readings?

This section recommends a series of titles that can help the reader become familiar with some basic aspects related to the general approach developed in the previous sections. For those readers who are already familiar with them, the references mentioned therein are suggested as complementary readings.

3.1 Relevance Theory

3.1.1 Introductions to RT

General presentations of RT may be found in different formats, from short summaries to full-length books, intended for diversified audiences, from complete newcomers to more advanced readers.

Blakemore (1992) is a reader-friendly introduction to Pragmatics, focusing on RT, accessible to readers with no specific previous knowledge. After describing the main tenets of the theory, the book contrasts its approach to different phenomena (such as implicature, speech acts and discourse coherence) to the approach taken by other pragmatic theories. Special attention is also paid to what has traditionally been considered as stylistic effects (in particular, metaphor and metonymy). The main limitation of the book lies in the fact that it was published before the second edition of Sperber and Wilson's (1995) *Relevance*, which introduced some essential refinements to the first edition (published in 1986), including a modification of the main Principle of Relevance.

Clark (2013) constitutes a much more updated, in-depth overview of RT. It is conceived of as a textbook, accessible to non-specialised readers, but will also be useful to more advanced researchers who are looking to develop an understanding of the post-*Relevance* (1995) developments of the theory. The basic theory-internal notions and its later extensions are explained in detail; two sections on linguistic semantics are included; one of them deals with the distinction between conceptual and procedural meaning, with clear characterisations and analyses. Each section of the book includes suggestions for further reading.

Any reader intending to go beyond the general features of the theory should read Sperber and Wilson (1995). However, short summaries of the model may be found in many Pragmatics handbooks. Wilson and Sperber (2004) and Sperber and Wilson (2005) will be useful to those readers looking for a compact, articulated approach to the main concepts and concerns of RT.

Over the years, many collective volumes on advances and developments of the relevance-theoretic framework have been published. To date, Scott et al. (2019) is possibly the most comprehensive and authoritative monography of this kind. Some key areas highlighted in that volume as recent developments of RT are the field of experimental pragmatics (for an overview of this area, see also Noveck and Sperber, 2004, and Breheny, 2011), the human capacity for epistemic vigilance (see also Sperber et al., 2010; Mazzarella, 2013; Reboul, 2017), lexical pragmatics (Wilson and Carston, 2007; Carston, 2012, 2013; Kolaiti and Wilson, 2014), the relation between pragmatics and theory of mind (Sperber and Wilson, 2002; Breheny, 2006), the relation between pragmatics and the evolution of language (Reboul, 2015; Scott-Philips, 2015), pragmatics and the stylistic analysis of texts (Caink and Clark, 2012; Chapman and Clark, 2014) and the development of pragmatic abilities in children (Papafragou and Tantalou, 2004; Pouscoulous, 2013; Zufferey, 2015).

3.1.2 Language and Linguistic Meaning in Relevance Theory

From its inception, RT has paid special attention to verbal phenomena that occur in human intentional communication. An internal concern of the theory has been how its perspective on language relates to current linguistic theory, particularly to generativist approaches to language and the mind. RT adopts a modular view of human cognitive architecture, and shares with generativist views certain basic principles, such as that of economy of derivation and representation. Both generativist linguistics and Relevance centre attention on sub-personal, algorithmic processes which are considered to be frequent in cognitive functioning. Parallelisms between RT and generativist views of language have been noted and explored in Carston (2000), Escandell-Vidal (2016), Allott and Wilson (2021), Guijarro-Fuentes et al. (2020), and Ahern et al. (2023b).

The relations between the linguistically encoded meanings studied in semantics and the thoughts that humans are capable of entertaining have received a great deal of attention among relevance theorists. Wilson and Sperber (2012) constitute a collection of fifteen previously published texts from both authors (written individually, together or in collaboration with others) on linguistic meaning and thought that have been deeply influential. One of the chapters from this collection, 'Linguistic form and Relevance' (Wilson and Sperber, 1993), is fundamental to the studies we have presented in this Element. Although the conceptual versus procedural distinction was first put forth in Blakemore (1987), Sperber and Wilson (1993) reshaped the distinction, widened its scope and established the main starting point for subsequent studies.

As mentioned in the previous sections, the conceptual versus procedural distinction has been approached in various ways by different researchers. Wilson (2016) offers a personal examination of how this distinction has evolved in RT after almost thirty years of research. Wilson reflects on the nature of procedural encoding and discusses whether it should be considered as semantic or pragmatic; she argues that procedural encoding is properly *semantic*, even though pragmatics is present in the application of specific interpretation procedures. She also argues that the conceptual–procedural distinction was not intended to be mutually exclusive, and that a single word can encode both types of meaning at the same time.

A more comprehensive, plural account of procedural meaning is found in Escandell-Vidal et al. (2011). The volume features fifteen chapters on procedural meaning written by different scholars. Within that book, Wilson's approach to mixed conceptual and procedural meaning is in partial contrast with the views of other researchers such as Saussure, Escandell-Vidal and Leonetti. In the latter approach, words are seen as bundles of semantic and syntactic features; some of the semantic features may be conceptual, while others are procedural. It is only in that sense that single expressions may contain conceptual and procedural meaning at the same time, but this does not imply that the two types of encoding may generate mixed semantic features (see also Escandell-Vidal, 2016).

RT has been very influential in the study of lexical semantics and its relationship with concepts (Carston, 1997; Sperber and Wilson, 1998; Wilson and Carston, 2007). In the RT account of lexical semantics, pragmatic effects on the meaning contributed by a word to the proposition expressed have been extensively studied. Processes of narrowing (cases where the extension of a word used in an utterance is less than the extension of the lexically encoded word) and broadening (cases where the contribution made by a word has a broader extension than the lexically encoded one) have been analysed in numerous works. Carston (2002) represented a major development in this line of research. In her book, Carston devoted a 45-page chapter to developing the notion of *ad-hoc* concepts and their role on on-line concept construction. *Ad-hoc* concepts are seen as occasional senses of words, in which only some relevant features of a concept are accessed and incorporated into the proposition expressed. The resulting concept may be narrower or wider than the original one. Carston's views on explicit communication and her contributions to RT are thoroughly explored in Soria and Romero's (2010) collective volume, in which fourteen chapters are brought together along three main thematical lines: the nature of lexically encoded meanings; the relevance-theoretic notion of explicature; the internal structure of explicature and the phenomena that contribute to it.

3.1.3 RT and Language Acquisition

Smith and Tsimpli (1995) and Smith et al. (2011) thoroughly build the case-study of Christopher, a *savant* with unusual language abilities. Associating generativist and relevance-theoretic conceptions of language and the mind, Smith, Tsimpli and colleagues provide evidence on the modularity of mind and motivate significant assumptions on how different mental functions interact in the acquisition and use of additional languages. Integrating linguistic and pragmatic information is particularly challenging for Christopher, partly because of the cognitive load entailed. However, as the authors themselves acknowledge, the specificity of Cristopher's case does not allow direct generalisations on SLA in non-clinical conditions.

Cognitive, relevance-theoretic compatible accounts of pragmatic abilities in first language acquisition are developed in Zufferey (2010, 2015, 2020). Also, in recent decades, several researchers have used the analytic tools of the relevance theoretical framework to describe and explain a number of L2 learning/acquisition phenomena. Most of these analyses have concentrated on how – and to what extent – the type of interpretation processes described in RT may apply to L2 utterances and how the study of those L2 interpretation processes may shed light on how language acquisition proceeds.

Paiva (2003), Paiva and Foster-Cohen (2004) and Foster Cohen (2004) study the development of pragmatic knowledge in L2, showing useful insights from RT on the processes involved in learners' perceptions of L2 input. Particularly, they claim that the relevance-theoretic framework has predictive explanatory power for analysing the role of attention and inferencing. Foster-Cohen (2000, 2004) argues that the cognitive mechanisms involved in understanding utterances in L1 and L2 are the same. Inferential capacities are common to the human species: interpreting an utterance systematically requires decoding and pragmatic enrichment, in accordance with the cognitive principle of relevance. Foster-Cohen pays attention to how L2 linguistic information is selected. She claims that L2 learners tend to concentrate on content words, disregarding purely grammatical information.

Analysing the effects of cognitive overload in L2 utterance processing, Garcés-Cornejos and Bou-Franch (2004, pp. 20–23) analyse the limitations of the L2 hearer building on Sperber's (1994) proposals. According to Garcés-Cornejos and Bou-Franch, the cognitive load leads the L2 hearer to concentrate on explicit information, avoiding the manipulation of supplementary mental representations. This strategy often leads to inadequate, incomplete or erroneous interpretations.

Liszka (2004) shows that analysing along relevance-theoretic lines some aspects of grammatical deficits in the L2 production of learners belonging to a specific native language background can explain the nature of the obstacles they face. She argues that if a certain linguistic feature is not available in their L1, an L2 learner might nevertheless access non-linguistic resources, such as encyclopaedic representations, and retrieve an approximation of the form required in the construction of an utterance aiming for optimal relevance. However, successful utterance interpretation and use would be more probabilistic than for native speakers who have the relevant feature specified in their grammars.

A different type of application of RT to the description of L2 acquisition processes is developed by Niżegorodcew (2007). She analyses the role of teacher's discourse in language learning in the L2 classroom and claims that L2 teachers' instructional input can change the level of expected optimal relevance from an automatic search for meaning to momentarily focusing on the code and adjusting one's interpretation to the original meaning of the message. This view that language instruction contexts – such as L2 lessons – lead to alternating the focus of expectations of relevance between the speaker's meaning and language forms is aligned with what Doughty (2001, p. 249) identifies as 'small cognitive windows of opportunity through which teachers can intervene focusing on form in otherwise meaning-focused activities'.

Amenós-Pons and Ahern (2017) focus on the potential significance of RT for L2 teacher education. They claim that the theory contains general features of great interest for the development of a reflective language teaching professional. These include: the concept of communication as an intentional activity; the non-exclusively linguistic nature of the stimuli; the notion of context as a mental construct of the speakers; the notion of scripts as culturally mediated structures of knowledge; the relationship between general cognitive capacities and communicative language competences. In addition, RT is built upon a notion of processing effort and cognitive economy, which may be related to current accounts of how L2 knowledge develops. The distinction between the basic properties of conceptual and procedural linguistic units has important consequences for their greater or lesser difficulty in L1 and L2. Finally, the process of developing L2 communicative competence involves exercising the learner's ability to form mental representations of the communicative situation and the language used, adjusting the individual expectations, social behaviour and their output or production of that language. RT affords a cognitively realistic model of human communication that helps to develop a deeper understanding of all these processes.

3.2 L2 Acquisition Models Compatible with RT

3.2.1 The Modular Cognition Framework

RT provides a detailed account of how the mind processes language and how the output of language processing is stored and accessed in the mind. The general principles of this model are expected to hold for any linguistic input, be it in an

L1 or an L2. No specific claims are made regarding L2 acquisition. Nevertheless, the cognitive underpinnings of RT (in particular, the postulate of a modular architecture of the mind) make it largely compatible with specific L2 acquisition models, especially to acquisition-by-processing theories such as the Modular Cognition Framework (MCF) (Sharwood Smith, 2017; Truscott and Sharwood Smith, 2019).

The MCF consists of a set of hypotheses about the cognitive architecture involved in mental processing and representation, which can act as a shared framework to embed theoretical and empirical research from different disciplines. Like RT, the MCF assumes that the mind is composed of expert systems that have evolved over time in order to optimally perform. This perspective emphasises the role of interfaces, conceived not as representational levels but as processing devices. Language, in its broadest sense, involves many different functionally specialised processing systems, each with its own (memory) store. Of these systems, only the phonological and syntactic systems constitute a language module as it would be conceived of within the framework of generative linguistics. Closely associated with these core systems is a rich set of conceptual structures developed throughout life, as well as auditory structures which have been paired with phonological structures and visual structures created to interpret writing and sign language. In addition, there are the various motor structures involved in the production of language in its different modalities.

Building on Jackendoff (2002), the MCF takes a particular view of the long-established Chomskyan distinction between competence and performance. On the MCF view, acquired linguistic structures are natural by-products of on-line processing. At any given moment, the human mind has sets of representations that may be used in producing or interpreting utterances. These representations can belong to different systems, where they are stored. The phonological and syntactic systems are the purely linguistic ones; they are adjoined, respectively, to the auditory and the conceptual systems. Each system includes a (memory) store where representations are placed and are more or less accessible depending on the degree to which they are activated.

Any of these representations may be activated to different degrees, depending on how recently and how repeatedly they have been processed. Representations that become activated are accessible to the working memory within the corresponding store. Each store follows particular processing principles which are applied to the representations that are activated. After the representation has been processed, that representation falls from the activated mode to a resting level, where it remains accessible to working memory to a slightly higher degree than it was at before it had been processed. The higher the resting level of a representation gets, the more accessible it will be. So regular, repeated activation of a representation makes it easily accessible to working memory.

Also, for a given task, different representations will be activated at the same time, which leads to competition. The activated representations may belong to a single language or to different languages; they compete to be selected for the task or purpose at hand. The perspective of acquisition by processing, adopted in the MCF, assumes that when a representation is applied in a task, an association is formed and as the same representation is accessed repeatedly and regularly, the association grows stronger and leads to more robust representations. The resting levels of any representations that are not accessed regularly and frequently will sink, that is, get lower over time and then will be less available for activation, and forgotten.

The purely linguistic systems are arranged as depicted in Figure 2, where we can see that the phonological and syntactic systems share an interface (they are placed together so it can be said, metaphorically, that their shared boundary forms an interface). The phonological system also interfaces with the auditory system; and the syntactic system, with the conceptual one. As Sharwood Smith (2021a, p. 4) explains, speech that is picked up by the auditory system will provide input to the phonological system, activating a phonological representation. This, in parallel, activates a representation in the syntactic system; development or, in other words, language acquisition is, on the MCF view, a result of regular processing mechanisms.

In adult L2 acquisition, the MCF assumes that UG elements are fully available, but any new instantiations, for example the selection of different parameter settings or alternative feature values, must compete with deep-rooted L1 representations. When the learner is in the process of acquiring an additional language (L2), this competition with more robustly developed representations from the first language(s) leads to variability in L2 production. The MCF suggests that the development of an L2 is best seen as a gradual progression from L1 values to L2 values, rather than as a succession of clear interlanguage stages.

In reference to clarifying the distinction between implicit and explicit knowledge of a language, the MCF is a helpful perspective. Sharwood Smith (2021b) explains that the language module – that is, the combination of PS and SS – is not directly involved in any explicit thinking about language, because these systems processing takes place at subconscious levels. Processing within the language module will always be automatically triggered by exposure to

acoustic input > AS ⟺ **PS** ⟺ **SS** ⟺ CS

Figure 2 MCF processing architecture (Sharwood Smith, 2021a, p. 4).

linguistic stimuli, whereas explicit metalinguistic activity is developed by the conceptual system, where meaning is represented. Nevertheless, the language module is crucial for all other types of linguistic activity and is vital in explaining language acquisition. Acquiring language can begin with pairing of auditory and conceptual representations, which will eventually build up into chains of representations that also include the phonological and syntactic representations. A fully developed representation of any word or linguistic expression will necessarily involve the abstract representations of the PP and the SS. No single activation of auditory and conceptual structure can explain the growth of language in the mind after repeated exposure to speech, which is most evident in the case of young children and (possibly) also in adults.

A person can possess an encyclopedic knowledge of the grammar of a particular language and yet be a very poor user of that language. We may have misconceptions about the language, or we may have a view of grammar that agrees with the facts. In contrast, the system that works subconsciously within our linguistic module can never be right or wrong: it is simply the way it is, the way it has developed over time in the human mind. It is above all the implicit knowledge of language that drives linguistic performance.

3.2.2 Processing Instruction Theory

When discussing the implications of RT for the field of L2 acquisition, Foster-Cohen (2000) recalls that this framework suggests that, guided by the Principle of Relevance, the non-native listener selects the information they consider most relevant to them in the accessed, seeking (like the native speaker) a balance between effort and cognitive performance. However, the non-native listener's selection is affected by the limitations of their linguistic knowledge, the characteristics of his encyclopedic knowledge and the processing limitations imposed by cognitive effort. Quoting VanPatten (1996), Foster-Cohen (2000) states that foreign language learners tend to select content words (i.e., conceptual expressions) rather than those containing purely grammatical information (procedural expressions), the meaning load of which is abstract and much less obvious.

Thus, VanPatten's Processing Instruction Theory makes predictions on L2 processing that may be compatible with the general principles of RT, as well as with the MCF framework (Sharwood-Smith and Truscott, 2014, p. 225). VanPatten's model was first described in VanPatten's (1996) book, and updated in VanPatten (2004). A summary of the model is given in VanPatten (2007).

Input Processing makes several claims about what guides L2 learners processing of linguistic data in the input they try to comprehend in the following principles (VanPatten, 2007):

- The Primacy of Content Word Principle: Learners process content words before anything else.
- The Lexical Preference Principle: Learners will process lexical items for meaning before grammatical items.
- The Lexical Preference Principle: If grammatical forms express a meaning that is also encoded lexically, the learners will not initially process those grammatical forms.
- The Preference for Nonredundancy Principle: Learners are more likely to process nonredundant meaningful grammatical markers before they process redundant meaningful markers.
- The Meaning before Nonmeaning Principle: Learners are more likely to process meaningful grammatical markers before nonmeaningful grammatical markers.
- The First Noun Principle: Learners tend to process the first noun or pronoun they encounter in a sentence as the subject.
- The L1 Transfer Principle: Learners begin acquisition with L1 parsing procedures.
- The Event Probability Principle: Learners may rely on event probabilities, where possible, instead of the First Noun Principle to interpret sentences.
- The Lexical Semantics Principle: Learners may rely on lexical semantics (or an L1 parsing procedure), instead of the First Noun Principle.
- The Contextual Constraint Principle: Learners may rely on the First Noun Principle if preceding context constrains the possible interpretations of a new clause of sentence.
- The Sentence Location Principle: Learners tend to process items in sentence initial position before those in final or medial position.

Over the years, VanPatten's model has generated abundant research, testing its hypotheses on different languages. A critical review of this research, with numerous references, is found in Rasuki (2017). VanPatten's general views on L2 acquisition are presented (by means of a 'key-questions' structure) in VanPatten et al. (2020). The roles of explicit and implicit learning in SLA, following VanPatten's view, are analysed in VanPatten and Smith (2022); the authors conclude that that SLA is largely (if not exclusively) implicit in nature and that explicit learning plays a secondary role.

3.2.3 Feature Reassembly Hypothesis

Pioneered by Lardiere (2008, 2009), Lardiere tries to move away from previous generative SLA hypotheses and proposes her FRH which catches in a more precise way the complexity of the form-meaning mapping task in SLA.

Departing from the basic question of what exactly gets transferred from the L1 into the L2, Lardiere assumes that L2 learners transfer into the L2 abstract units of meaning, or linguistic features, expressed by L1 words and morphemes. As mentioned in the previous sections, the FRH is a theoretical approach according to which linguistic information is associated with feature bundles and functional heads. Successful reassembly thus involves the reassignment of feature bundles to different functional heads. This view assumes that all lexical items, that is, words and morphemes, are physical realisations of grammatical and semantic features. Even though the atomic units of meaning or linguistic features are universal, languages are different in how they organise them into words and morphemes (see Section 1).

Since its implementation numerous studies in the field have adopted it given that the FRH pioneers conceptualisation of L1 transfer as an initial step by L2 learners to determine a direct mapping between L1 and L2 forms. The FRH is particularly appropriate to the study of L2 development because it predicts that when a one-to-one initial mapping is unsuccessful, L2 learners will gradually reorganise the L1 grammatical system until they attain (possibly complete) convergence. That said, FRH predicts that initially L1 transfer operates in a very straightforward manner enabling an L2 learner to look for one-to-one correspondences/matches between L1 and L2 forms (namely, the MAPPING stage). However, when that mapping stage is not possible due to multiple reasons including the differences between language features, L1 feature bundles need to be gradually reassembled to match new L2 meanings (namely, the REASSEMBLY stage).

For our purposes, in some of our own studies we have explored how L1-L2 (mis)matches in linguistic features affect language acquisition by different populations, thereby extending the application of the FRH beyond the acquisition of grammatical representations adopting some of the basic tenets of the RT. In other words, if and when L2 learners reconfigure linguistic features into new L2 words, can they automatically use the information conveyed by L2 words to correctly produce and comprehend the L2?[4]

3.2.4 Interface Hypothesis

In 2011, Antonella Sorace, in her keynote epistemological paper published in *Linguistic Approaches to Bilingualism* (entitled 'Pinning down the concept of "Interface" in bilingualism') and later in her reply to her peers in 2012, outlines

---

[4] Space limitations prevent us from reviewing past and recent research that has expanded the FRH to semantic features (e.g., Diaubalick and Guijarro-Fuentes, 2019; Domínguez, Arche and Myles, 2017; Guijarro-Fuentes and Pires, 2023; Marsden, 2009, to name just a few).

the basic tenets of the Interface Hypothesis that she together with her associated had been working on for quite some time. The Interface Hypothesis has attracted a lot of attention within the field, and some of the papers that are reviewed herein are not aware of it either.

Concretely, drawing from results from previous and selective research on several linguistic phenomena such as the use of overt versus null subjects, as well as the use of subject placement before or after the verb to mark focus versus the use of prosody, in Romance languages as Italian by native English speakers, Sorace made certain claims among which for adult second language learners, acquiring grammatical properties within a given linguistic area, such as phonology, syntax or semantics should not be problematic. Interfacing between those modules, such as communicating between the syntax and semantic systems, should likewise be feasible. Nevertheless, grammatical operations where the L2 speaker or alike is required to interface between an internal component of the grammar and an external component, such as pragmatics or discourse information, will prove to be very difficult and will not be completely acquired by the second language learner, even at very advanced levels. In Sorace (2011, 2012), the author tries to put right some of the misunderstandings around her hypothesis, and at the same times outlines some interdisciplinary and methodological developments to move the language acquisition agenda forwards.

As mentioned in the previous section, the Interface Hypothesis has been extended to other language scenario including first language acquisition (e.g., Guijarro-Fuentes and Rothman, 2012 and references therein) and to the very early stages of first language attrition. In sum, this approach provides the tools for the examination of language acquisition development[5].

3.3 Pragmatic Competence in L2

Within the literature on L2 development, the term *pragmatic competence* has largely been analysed as a socially grounded body of knowledge that an individual may possess, which includes aspects such as an understanding of the conditions of appropriateness of speech acts for particular situations and purposes; the manifestations of politeness characteristic of a community; the judgments usually accorded to specific linguistic behaviour within the community of the target language speakers (see González-Lloret, 2020 for an overview).

Within this general basis, however, the concept of pragmatic competence has evolved over time. The concept was first defined by Canale and Swain (1980) who, in their model of communicative competence, situated pragmatic competence as

---

[5] Nevertheless, as stated in Section 2.3, some studies have also uncovered behaviour that runs counter the Interface Hypothesis proposal.

a specific sub-competence, distinct from grammatical, discursive and strategic competences. In Europe, this line of thought crystallised at the beginning of the present century with the publication of the *European Framework of Reference for Languages* (CEFR) (Council of Europe, 2001). In the formulation of the CEFR, pragmatic competence includes the handling of communicative functions (a concept directly related to speech act theory) and discourse typologies. However, another aspect traditionally studied by pragmatics, politeness, is integrated into what the CEFR calls *sociolinguistic competence*.

The evolution of the concept of pragmatic competence in L2 teaching clearly reflects the rise of discourse pragmatics (Kasper, 2006). It is now accepted that form-function-context associations depend on the development of the inter-action and are jointly constructed between the participants in the discourse. Moreover, form-function-context associations are constantly changing as a function of changing contextual dynamics, such as speakers' attitudes, affect and discourse direction.

In recent decades, the development of cross-cultural pragmatics (Kecskes, 2014, 2016) has broadened our understanding of what being pragmatically competent entails. Kecskes proposed a socio-cognitive approach, which on the one hand considers intention as pre-existing in the mind of the speaker before it is uttered, and, on the other hand, takes into account a socio-cultural-interactional perspective, where intention is understood as an emergent prop-erty, jointly constructed by discourse participants. They rely on their own norms and expectations, but norms are negotiated and redefined as the participants seek common ground during interaction.

Hence, learners' willingness to suspend their own norms and seek mutual norms is a fundamental aspect of pragmatic competence. Intercultural pragmat-ics has highlighted the importance of the concept of agency, understood as a self-defining capacity that works with volition to bring about a certain effect on or change to one's behaviour (LoCastro, 2003). Thus, the concept of pragmatic competence extends to the analysis of how participants in intercul-tural communication events co-construct specific pragmatic norms with others, and how they appropriate others' norms and adapt their own.

However, RT takes a different approach, in concentrating on inferential abilities and cognitive processes as its primary focus of research, rather than social interaction phenomena. The inferential capacity is part of the genetically specified human endowment. Inference, of course, does not operate 'in a vacuum'. It is fed by socio-cultural data, filtered through language abilities and world knowledge. The implications of this shift for the study of L2 acquisition has been discussed by Ifantidou (2014, 2022) and Amenós-Pons et al. (2019). Assuming that languages are indispensable for information processing (and not for communication), Ifantidou (2014) highlights the importance of developing in the L2 learner the ability to process implicatures when interacting with L2 reading materials. Similarly, Amenós-Pons et al. (2019) highlight that developing L2 pragmatics implies paying attention to a social body of knowledge, but also to the cognitive capacities underpinning it, that is, the inferential mechanisms. The proper functioning of these mechanisms depends, in part, on the greater or lesser ease of access to the information needed to build appropriate inferences. Often, when using an L2, this functioning is greatly impaired by the cognitive effort involved. Reducing that effort depends, above all, on the learner's familiarity with the L2, that is, on the amount of input that a learner receives and on the opportunities the learner has to use it in authentic communication, and in a meaningful, socially and cognitively relevant way.

It is generally accepted that the development of L2 pragmatic abilities is directly linked to the development of other aspects of language: L2 learners start with a limited set of pragmalinguistic features; there is a general initial tendency to associate each L2 form to a single function. The longer the instruction time and the richer and more socially meaningful the input received by the learners, the higher their proficiency. Classic, well-known accounts of L2 pragmatic development are given by Rose and Kasper (2001) and Kasper and Rose (2002). For a more recent, updated summary of research findings, see Taguchi and Roever (2017) and Taguchi (2019).

4 Concluding Remarks: New Avenues for Research and Implications for Language Teaching

In this final section, we outline some current and potential developments of our approach, concerning both the study of L2 acquisition processes and the teaching of additional languages.

4.1 Language Outside the Language Module

As early as the 1950s, Noam Chomsky argued for the mentalistic character of human language; its essence, for Chomsky, lies in syntax, that is, in the innate capacity to combine, in a recursive and potentially unlimited way, a series of finite elements from a limited set of rules. Chomsky's theories have deeply influenced psychology, philosophy and neuroscience over recent decades. In particular, the assumption that the human mind is modular (Fodor, 1983; Jackendoff, 1997; Pinker, 1997, and references thereafter) has contributed to ideas on the nature of language. It is now widely assumed that the mind comprises a set of processors or modules, each handling data related to a different type of stimulus, as upheld in the Modular Cognition Framework (see Section 3.2.1).

For Chomsky, the linguistic module is a mental organ, the fruit of human evolution. The modular architecture of the mind sequentially is also a product of evolution: having a set of processors specialised in specific types of stimuli increases the speed and efficiency of information processing. The ability to relate different types of information depends on interface mechanisms between the different modules; the overall functioning of the system, in sequence, is the responsibility of the general cognitive systems.

In the generative conception, the production and interpretation of utterances depends not only on the data provided by the language module, but also on the processing of non-linguistic stimuli and the attribution of social meanings. For decades, however, the focus of generative linguistics was the description of the language faculty in the strict sense, that is, syntactic knowledge. Conversely, since the 1970s, other researchers have focused on the interaction of the language abilities with other cognitive components.

In the field of linguistics, this endeavour has followed two parallel and, to a large extent, alternative paths. On the one hand, a set of theories denies the existence of a language-specific module: these include the different approaches classified under the denomination of cognitive linguistics (Langacker, 1987, 1991; Lakoff, 1990; Goldberg, 1995, inter alia). For cognitive linguistics, language is the exclusive product of general cognitive abilities and develops from basic processes such as perception, attention and categorisation; grammar emerges only as a result of the fixation and abstraction of a series of frequent patterns of use, also described as a result of domain-general learning.

A second path, essentially different from the one just mentioned, is the view upheld, for instance, in RT. Sperber and Wilson do not reject the conceptual bases of generative linguistics, but rather deepen some of its proposals, among them the modular conception of the mind. RT (Sperber and Wilson, 1986/1995) was the first pragmatic theory that declared itself both cognitivist and modularist. Thus, building on the theories of Fodor (1983), Sperber and Wilson (1986/1995) initially conceive of the human mind as a set of systems specialised in processing specific types of information, coordinated by central systems of thought (responsible for inferential capacities). In more recent formulations of the theory, and following developments in the field of cognitive science, the importance of the modular architecture of the mind is further emphasised and the mere existence of core processes has been questioned (Sperber and Wilson, 2004).

In the proposals of RT, therefore, the levels of linguistic and pragmatic analysis are kept distinct; each level is related to a specific type of competence. However, and as we have shown in previous sections, in the interpretation of utterances, linguistic and non-linguistic information are considered to be systematically combined through inferential processes. This entails that in verbal communication, not only the language faculty comes into play, but also a variety of other types of knowledge, including social knowledge about people's identities and culturally grounded expectations on stereotypical ways that situations unfold through verbal interaction. For instance, the perception of register and, more generally, of the socio-pragmatic appropriateness of any given utterance to a communicative situation do not depend directly on phonological, lexical and morphosyntactic processing, but have to do with the particular uses of language and the social purpose they are associated with. The ability to adapt one's own linguistic production pragmatically (and to judge the pragmatic adequacy of the production of others), then, is based on knowledge acquired through socialisation (Escandell-Vidal, 2004).

4.2 Experimental Approaches to Language and Cognition

We have claimed in the preceding sections that the acquisition of procedural expressions in an L2 is always costly. This is to be expected especially for uses of procedural expressions whose interpretation requires complex interaction of linguistic and pragmatic information, because of the cognitive load involved. This is a claim that can be empirically tested, and the studies we have reviewed in the preceding sections have already begun to do so.

The RT approach to language, and more specifically, the RT description of pragmatic enrichment processes, has clear similarities with specific proposals developed or adopted in cognitive linguistics. This is illustrated, for example, in the RT analysis of how contextual assumptions are accessed as part of the utterance interpretation process, highlighting the role of cognitive scripts (see Kövecses, 2006 for a detailed cognitive linguistics-based introduction to this notion). As Carston (2002, p. 226) puts it:

> it is widely assumed in cognitive studies that frequently experienced actions, events or processes and sequences of these are stored in chunks, as frames or scripts. Some of these may be relatively specific [...]. These are stereotypical scenarios which are clearly acquired through experience. Others may be of a more skeletal or abstract nature, such as that humans generally perform actions with a purpose in mind, or that events in the world are usually causally connected to other events; these may have a more fundamental cognitive status, perhaps originating as part of innately given domain-specific capacities.

When interpreting utterances, stereotypical scripts are often accessed and used as background assumptions. The RT comprehension strategy provides an explanation for this fact: the hearer constructs the most accessible interpretation (which in many cases will be the stereotypical one) and, if it satisfies their expectation of relevance, the search stops there.

The RT notion of context and the way RT accounts for how context is accessed can substantiate other cognitive accounts on how linguistic and not-linguistic information interact in the interpretation of utterances. RT proposals on this interaction are specific, so they can be experimentally tested. Testing theoretical claims using psycholinguistic techniques has been one of the main contributions of experimental pragmatics, a fast-developing, RT-inspired field brought to fruition through the work of Noveck and colleagues (Noveck and Posada, 2003; Bott and Noveck, 2004).

Over recent decades, the study of different types of implicatures and the contextual factors that modulate the availability of implicature in online pro-cessing has been the focus of many experimental pragmatics studies (see Gibbs, 2017; Cummins and Katsos, 2019 for overviews). Implicatures are related to what RT calls semantic narrowing or widening, that is, processes of contextual modulation of lexically encoded meaning. Experimental studies have provided evidence of two types of inferencing: *voluntary* and *imposed* (Noveck, 2018). Voluntary inferences are those where the linguistically encoded meaning 'can provide an interpretation that is good enough, but that can also lead with extra effort, and if the listener so chooses, to a more informative reading'. Contrastingly, imposed inferences correspond to 'cases in which a speaker practically requires the addressee to enrich an aspect of an utterance in order to provide an approximation of the speaker's intended meaning'. According to Noveck (2018), the contrast between voluntary and imposed processes has been seen to play a role in seemingly unrelated interpretation phenomena; for instance, interpreting novel metaphors or understanding conditional sentences are cases of imposed inference, while interpreting the chronological structure of a series of events is an example of voluntary inference.

Experimental approaches will undoubtedly continue to develop in the future. They can be expected to continue to provide empirical evidence substantiating theoretical considerations about the nature of language and interpretation pro-cesses. Experimental research on how linguistic and extralinguistic knowledge interact in the human mind has recently become essential for developing artificial intelligence-based text generating systems. These systems can already generate increasingly human-like text as they can integrate information on the context, implicatures and sociolinguistic variables in the use and interpretation of language.

4.3 Some Implications for Theory and Practice in Language Teaching

The interactions among grammatical, semantic and pragmatic factors at the interfaces that have been explored in the previous sections have implications that link them to theories of SLA and particularly, acquisition by processing perspectives. The RT distinction between the basic properties of conceptual and procedural expressions can help explain challenges in learning different types of expressions in L1 and L2.

We acquire procedural expressions in our L1s through implicit learning from the abundant input we are exposed to in childhood, and long before the ability to reason about or explain them develops. In fact, since procedural expressions support conceptual representations (Sperber, 1996), they can be likened to the nails, nuts and bolts or hinges that articulate and hold together the lexical words representing concepts and which stand out as what carries meaning. So, for L2 learners, these expressions are difficult to notice, understand and use accurately because of their abstract nature (Escandell-Vidal, 2006). This idea is intuitively clear: for a learner, it is in principle easier to learn the lexical meaning of a group of new words than to effectively and accurately use verb tenses, know when it's more appropriate to use a stressed pronoun or an empty one in a pro-drop language, or effectively highlight information through fronting for topicalisation. Likewise, using lexical verbs to convey possibility or commitment to the truth of a proposition is simpler than attempting to differentiate well the uses of indicative and subjunctive, especially in environments where both are possible, and alternation between these verbal moods is linked to intentional aspects.

Thus, the distinction between conceptual and procedural meanings can inform pedagogical decisions concerning the segmentation of language content into different levels of learning, as it helps to better understand how lexis and grammar are related in the individual's mind and to ascertain why certain aspects are more complex than others.

In the process of interpretation, as has been mentioned, words act as clues that the addressee must complete, disambiguate, and enrich to varying degrees with linguistic and extralinguistic contextual information. RT has highlighted the importance of an individual's mental representations in the interpretation of utterances. Part of these representations are social frames or scripts, that is, stereotyped sets of knowledge, shared widely by members of a community. Scripts allow us to have expectations of what will happen and how a social situation of interaction will unfold. The way in which RT describes the contextual enrichment of lexical meanings has clear implications for L2 teaching, linked to the relationship between language and culture. Clearly, part of the contextual enrichment of any lexical expression is cultural in nature[6]. Thus, in different languages, words with superficially equivalent meanings may be associated with significantly different representations, depending on the social practices connected with the concept in question. As Escandell (2014) points out, the contribution of lexical units is not limited exclusively to encoding a concept; these units also lead into encyclopaedic information and the cultural expectations associated with it. When the cultural expectations surrounding these concepts are different from the ones in the speaker's culture of origin, their use in the target language is likely to give rise, in the initial stages of learning, to cross-linguistic / cross-cultural effects that may be a source of misunderstanding.

Describing the inferential process applied in interpreting an utterance, including how contextual assumptions are integrated into the process and impact on the meaning that is identified, leads to a lengthy and cumbersome explanation. This is analogous to the conceptualised representation of procedural expressions that an L2 learner must operate with until they become able to use them in a native-like way. In addition, until L2 proficiency builds up through using the target language enough (processing input and producing the language for communicative purposes) the pre-existing L1 knowledge remains more accessible and 'gets in the way' of the cognitive processing mechanisms (Sharwood Smith, 2019). This leads to cross-linguistic influences that interfere with fluent L2 communication. The RT distinction between conceptual and procedural meaning, in addition, finds a parallelism in a perspective on SLA that was developed independently from cognitive pragmatic accounts: the declarative versus procedural memory contrast (Ullman, 2016; DeKeyser, 2020).

According to Ullman's research (see Ullman, 2016), in L2 acquisition, declarative memory is where new learning is stored and it relies on metalinguistic knowledge like, for instance, conscious learning of grammar rules. The spontaneous use of language and the result of implicit learning, on the other hand, activates knowledge stored in what is labelled procedural memory (Ullman's use of the term 'procedural' refers is somewhat more restrictive and different from the notion it refers to within RT). This author has compiled neurolinguistic evidence of the declarative-procedural memory distinction,

---

[6] In studies on intercultural communication there has been an evolution in the concept of culture, from the essentialist view that associated one culture with one nation, to non-essentialist views that consider it to be made up of a variety of identity markers, beyond nationality: gender, sexuality, religion, race, class, political affiliation, education and so on (Dervin, 2016; Risager, 2018; Hoff, 2020). In bringing these elements together under the umbrella of culture, to consider its role in the RT conception of the cognitive environment shows how communication by speakers of different languages and who belong to different cultures becomes exponentially more complex.

which has been influential in a range of SLA research (Rastelli, 2023 provides an overview).

As suggested by VanPatten and Smith (2022), taking stock of SLA research findings points to the general conclusion that implicit learning is the main path to effective development of second or additional languages. This conclusion is consistent with the views purported by RT on the cognitive architecture involved in ostensive-inferential communication, where implicit processes are the core mechanisms that enable us to use language efficiently.

In sum, although RT is not, in principle, a framework designed to describe L2 acquisition but a general theory on human intentional communication, many RT concepts are compatible with certain acquisition theories or models.

On the other hand, when it comes to pedagogical implications, the observations and analyses we have provided evidently support approaches to teaching that take into consideration the important role of implicit learning (Long, 2014; Benati, 2021; VanPatten and Smith, 2022). Even though explicit instruction is a reliable way to reinforce or speed up implicit acquisition, the pragmatic mechanisms that have been described throughout this Element suggest how cognitive processing is complex and, at the same time, usually unconscious. As a basic premise for classroom instruction, we should not lose sight of this, even though instruction necessarily relies on declarative knowledge.

References

Adger, D. (2021). On doing theoretical linguistics. *Theoretical Linguistics* 47, 33–45.

Adger, D. (1993). The licensing of Quasi-arguments. In P. Ackema and M. Schoorlemmer (eds.), *Proceedings of Console*, vol. 1, pp. 1–18. The Hague: Holland Academic Graphics.

Adger, D. and Svenonius, P. (2011). Features in minimalist syntax. In C. Boeckx (ed.), *Oxford Handbook of Linguistic Minimalism*, pp. 27–51. Oxford: Oxford University Press.

Ahern, A., Amenós-Pons, J., and Guijarro-Fuentes, P. (2014). Interfaces in the interpretation of mood alternation in L2 Spanish: Morpho-phonology, semantics and pragmatics. In L. Roberts, I. Vedder and J. H. Hulstijn (eds.), *EuroSLA Yearbook 2014*, pp. 173–200. Amsterdam: John Benjamins.

Ahern, A., Amenós-Pons, J., and Guijarro-Fuentes, P. (2016). Mood interpretation in Spanish: Towards an encompassing view of L1 and L2 interface variability. In P. Guijarro-Fuentes and and M. Juan-Garau (eds.), *Acquisition of Romance Languages. Old Acquisition Challenges and New Explanations from a Generative Perspective*, pp. 141–170. Berlín: De Gruyter Mouton.

Ahern, A., Amenós-Pons, J., and Guijarro-Fuentes, P. (2020). Future tense acquisition by French-speaking learners of L2 Spanish: Chronology, conjecture and concession. In P. Guijarro-Fuentes and C. Suárez-Gómez (eds.), *New Trends in Language Acquisition Within the Generative Perspective*. Studies in Theoretical Psycholinguistics, vol. 49, pp. 27–48. Dordrecht: Springer.

Ahern, A., Amenós-Pons, J., and Guijarro-Fuentes, P. (2023a). Conjectural future in French and in Spanish: An L2 acquisition perspective. In M. Carretero, J. Marín-Arrese, E. Dominguez-Romero and V. Martín de la Rosa (eds.), *Evidentiality and Epistemic Modality: Conceptual and Descriptive Issues*, pp. 172–199. Berna: Peter Lang.

Ahern, A., Amenós-Pons, J., and Guijarro-Fuentes, P. (2023b). Relevance theory and the study of linguistic interfaces in second language acquisition. *Intercultural Pragmatics* 20(4), 429–453.

Ahern, A., Amenós-Pons, J., and Guijarro-Fuentes, P. (2023c). Expressing evidentiality in two languages: Conjectural future in Catalan/Spanish bilinguals, In J. Marín Arrese, L. Hidalgo-Downing and J. R. Zamorano-Mansilla (eds.), *Stance, Inter/Subjectivity and Identity in Discourse*, pp. 127–150. Berna: Peter Lang.

Allott, N. and Wilson, D. (2021). Chomsky and pragmatics. In N. Allott, T. Lohndal and G. Rey (eds.), *A Companion to* Chomsky, pp. 433–448. Hoboken, NJ: Wiley Blackwell.

Amenós-Pons, J. (2010). *Los tiempos de pasado del español y el francés: semántica, pragmática y aprendizaje de E/LE*. PhD dissertation. Madrid, UNED.

Amenós-Pons, J. (2011). Cross-linguistic variation in procedural expressions: Semantics and pragmatics. In V. Escandell-Vidal, M. Leonetti and A. Ahern (eds.), *Procedural Meaning: Problems and Perspectives*, pp. 235–266. Bingley: Emerald.

Amenós-Pons, J. (2015). Spanish 'imperfecto' vs. French 'imparfait' in hypothetical clauses: A procedural account. *Cahiers Chronos* 27, 235–66.

Amenós-Pons, J. (2023). Significados procedimentales, enriquecimiento contextual y variación geolectal: en torno al perfecto compuesto (y el perfecto simple). *Revista Española de Lingüística* 53/2, 81–116.

Amenós-Pons, J., Ahern, A. and Guijarro-Fuentes, P. (2019). Feature reassembly across closely related languages: L1 French vs. L1 Portuguese learning of L2 Spanish Past Tenses. *Language Acquisition* 26(2), 183–209.

Amenós-Pons, J. and Ahern, A. (2017). La pragmática cognitiva. Aportaciones para la formación de profesores de ELE. In D. G. Nikleva (ed.), *Necesidades y tendencias en la formación del profesorado de español como lengua extranjera*, pp. 155–202. Berlin: Peter Lang.

Amenós-Pons, J., Ahern, A., and Escandell-Vidal, V. (2019). *Comunicación y cognición en ELE: la perspectiva pragmática*. Madrid: Edinumen.

Aramon i Serra, R. (1957). Notes sobre alguns calcs sintàctics en l'actual català literari. *Syntactica* 1957, 1–31.

Archangeli, D. (1988). Underspecification in phonology. *Phonology* 5, 183–207.

Austin, J. L. (1962). *How to do Things with Words*, 2nd ed. Cambridge, MA: Harvard University Press.

Baker, M. (2008). The macroparameter in a microparametric world. In T. Biberauer (ed.), *The Limits of Syntactic Variation*, pp. 351–373. Amsterdam: John Benjamins.

Baron-Cohen, S. (2005). The empathizing system: A revision of the 1994 model of the mindreading system. In B. Ellis and D. Bjorklund (eds.), *Origins of the Social Mind*, pp. 468–492. New York: Guilford Publications.

Belleti, A., Bennati, E., and Sorace, A. (2007). Theoretical and developmental issues in the syntax of subjects: Evidence from near-native Italian. *Natural Language and Linguistic Theory*, 25, 657–689.

Belletti, A. (2004). *Structures and Beyond: Volume 3: The Cartography of Syntactic Structures*. Oxford, Oxford University Press.

Benati, A. (2021). *Focus on Form*. Cambridge: Cambridge University Press.

Blakemore, D. (1987). *Semantic Constraints on Relevance*. Oxford, Blackwell.

Blakemore, D. (1992). *Understanding Utterances*. Oxford, Blackwell.

Borer, H. (2003) . Exo-skeletal vs. endo-skeletal explanations: Syntactic projections and the lexicon. In J. Moore and M. Polinsky (eds.), *The Nature of Explanation in Linguistic Theory*, pp. 31–65. Chicago: University of Chicago Press.

Borgonovo, C., Bruhn de Garavito, J., and Prévost, P. (2005). Acquisition of mood distinctions in L2 Spanish. In A. Burgos, M. R. Clark-Cotton and S. Ha (eds.), *Proceedings of the 29th Boston University Conference on Language Development*, pp. 97–108. Somerville, MA: Cascadilla Press.

Borgonovo, C., Bruhn de Garavito, J., and Prévost, P. (2006). Is the semantics/ syntax interface vulnerable in L2 acquisition? Focus on mood distinctions clauses in L2 Spanish. In V. Torrens and L. Escobar (eds.), *The Acquisition of Syntax in Romance Languages*, pp. 353–69. Amsterdam: John Benjamins.

Borgonovo, C., Bruhn de Garavito, J., Guijarro-Fuentes, P., Prévost, P., and Valenzuela, E. (2006). Specificity in Spanish: The syntax/semantics interface in SLA. In S. Foster-Cohen and M. Medved Krajnovic (eds.), *Eurosla Yearbook 2006*, pp. 57–78. Amsterdam, John Benjamins.

Bos, P. Hollebrandese, B., and Sleeman, P. (2004). The pragmatics-syntax and the semantics-syntax interface in acquisition. *IRAL* 42, 101–10.

Bosque, I. (2016). Los rasgos gramaticales. In A. Gallego (ed.), *Perspectivas de sintaxis* formal, pp. 309–87. Madrid: Akal.

Bott, L. and Noveck, I. A. (2004). Some utterances are underinformative: The onset and time course of scalar inferences. *Journal of Memory and Language* 51(3), 437–457.

Breheny, R. (2006). Communication and Folk Psychology. *Mind and Language* 21–1, 74–107.

Breheny, R. (2011). Experimental pragmatics. In W. Bublitz and N. R. Norrick (eds.), *Foundations of* Pragmatics, pp. 551–86. Berlin: De Gruyter.

Bruhn de Garavito, J. and Valenzuela, E. (2006). Interpretive deficit? Evidence from the future tense in L2 Spanish. In J. Camacho, N. Flores-Ferrán, L. Sánchez, V. Déprez and M. J. Cabrera (eds.), *Romance Linguistics 2006: Selected papers from the 36th Linguistic Symposium on Romance Languages*, pp. 43–56. Amsterdam/Philadelphia: John Benjamins.

Caink, A. and Clark, B. (2012). Inference and implicature in literary interpretation. *Special Issue of Journal of Literary Semantics* 41(2), 88–191.

Canale, M. and Swain, M. (1980). Theoretical bases of communicative approaches to second language teaching and testing. *Applied Linguistics* 1, 1–47.

Canestrelli, A., Mak, W. and Sanders, T. (2013). Causal connectives in discourse. How differences in subjectivitiy are reflected in eye movements. *Language and Cognitive Processes* 28/9, 1394–413.

Carminati, M. N. (2002). *The Processing of Italian Subject Pronouns*. PhD Thesis, University of Massachusetts Amherst.

Carminati, M. N. (2005). Processing reflexes of the feature hierarchy (Person>Number>Gender) and implications for linguistic theory. *Lingua* 115, 259–285.

Carruthers, P. (2006). The case for massively modular models of mind. In R. J. Stainton (ed.), *Contemporary Debates in Cognitive Science*, pp. 3–21. London: Blackwell.

Carston, R. (1997). Enrichment and loosening: Complementary processes in deriving the proposition expressed? *Linguistische Berichte* 8, 103–127.

Carston, R. (2000). The relationship between generative grammar and (relevance-theoretic) pragmatics. *Language and Communication* 20, 87–103.

Carston, R. (2002). *Thoughts and Utterances: The Pragmatics of Explicit Communication*. Oxford: Blackwell.

Carston, R. (2012). Word meaning and concept expressed. *The Linguistic Review* 29(4), 607–23.

Carston, R. (2016). Linguistic conventions and the role of pragmatics. *Mind and Language* 31(5), 612–24.

Carston, R. A. (2013). Word meaning, what is said and explicature. In C. Penco and F. Domaneschi (eds.), *What Is Said and What Is Not*, pp. 175–203. Stanford: CSLI Publications.

Chapman, S. and Clark, B. (eds.) (2014). *Pragmatic Literary Stylistics*. New York, Palgrave Macmillan.

Chierchia, G., Guasti, M. T., Gualmini, A., Meroni, L., Crain, S. and Foppolo, F. (2004). Semantic and pragmatic competence in children's and adults' Comprehension of or. In I. Noveck and D. Sperber (eds.), *Experimental Pragmatics*, pp. 283–300. New York: Palgrave McMillan.

Chomsky, N. (1957). *Syntactic Structures*. The Hague/Paris: Mouton.

Chomsky, N. (1981). *Lectures on Government and Binding*. Dordrecht: Foris Publications .

Chomsky, N. (1982). *Some Concepts and Consequences of the Theory of Government and Binding*. Cambridge, MA: MIT Press.

Chomsky, N. (1995). *The Minimalist Program*. Cambridge, MA: MIT Press.

Chomsky, N. (2000). Minimalist inquiries: The framework. In R. Martin, D. Michaels, J. Uriagereka and S. J. Keyser (eds.), *Step by Step. Minimalist Essays in Honor of Howard Lasnik*, pp. 89–155. Cambridge, MA: MIT Press.

Chomsky, N. (2001). Beyond explanatory adequacy. *MIT Working Papers in Linguistics* 20, 1–28.

Chomsky, N. (2001). Derivation by phase. In M. Kenstowics (ed.), *Ken Hale: A life in language*, pp. 1–52. Cambridge, MA: MIT Press.

Chomsky, N. (2007). Approaching UG from below. In U. Sauerland and H.-M. Gärtner (eds.), *Interfaces + Recursion = Grammar? Chomsky's Minimalism and the View from Syntax- Semantics*, vol. 89, pp. 1–30. Berlin, Germany: Mouton de Gruyter.

Cinque, G. (1990). *Types of A'-dependencies*. Cambridge, MA: MIT Press.

Clahsen, H. and Muysken, P. (1986). The availability of Universal Grammar to adult and child learners: A study of the acquisition of German word order. *Second Language Research, 2*, 93–119.

Clark, B. (2013). *Relevance Theory*. Cambridge: Cambridge University Press.

Clements, G. N. and Hume, E. (1995). The internal organization of speech sounds. In J. Goldsmith (ed.), *The Handbook of Phonological Theory*, pp. 245–306. London: Blackwell.

Clements, G. N. (1985). The geometry of phonological features. *Phonology Yearbook* 2, 225–252.

Council of Europe (2001). *Common European Framework of Reference for Languages: Learning, Teaching, Assessment*. Strasbourg: Council of Europe.

Cummins, C., and Katsos, N. (eds.) (2019). *The Oxford Handbook of Experimental Semantics and Pragmatics*. Oxford: Oxford University Press.

de Saussure, L., and Morency, P. (2012). A cognitive-pragmatic view of the French epistemic future. *French Language Studies* 22, 207–23.

de Saussure, L. (2003). *Temps et pertinence: éléments de pragmatique cognitive du temps*. Brussels: De Boeck/Duculot.

de Saussure, L. (2011). On some methodological issues in the conceptual/ procedural distinction. In V. Escandell-Vidal, M. Leonetti, and A. Ahern (eds.), *Procedural meaning: Problems and perspectives*, pp. 55–79. Bingley: Emerald.

de Saussure, L. (2013). Perspectival interpretations of tenses. In K. M. Jaszczolt and L. de Saussure (eds.), *Time, Language, Cognition and Reality*, pp. 46–69. Oxford: Oxford University Press.

DeKeyser, R. M. (2020). Skill acquisition theory. In B. VanPatten, G. D. Keating, and S. Wulff, (eds.), *Theories in Second Language Acquisition*, pp. 83–104. New York, Routledge.

Dekydtspotter, L. and Sprouse, R. A. (2001). Mental design and (second) language epistemology: Adjectival restrictions of *wh*-quantifiers and tense in English-French interlanguage. *Second Language Research* 17, 1–35.

Dekydtspotter, L., Sprouse, R. A. and Thyre, R. (1999/2000). The interpretation of quantification at a distance in English-French interlanguage: Domain specificity and second language acquisition. *Language Acquisition* 8, 265–320.

Demonte, V. (2008). Meaning-form correlations and the order of adjectives in Spanish. En C. Kennedy and L. McNally (eds.), *The Semantics of Adjectives and Adverbs*, pp. 71–100. Oxford: Oxford University Press.

Dervin. F. (2016). *Interculturality in Education: A Theoretical and Methodological Toolbox*. London: Palgrave.

Diaubalick, T. and Guijarro-Fuentes, P. (2019). The strength of L1-effects on tense and aspect: How German learners of L2 Spanish deal with acquisitional problems. *Language Acquisition* 26(3), 282–301.

Domínguez, L., Arche, M. J., and Myles, F. (2017). Spanish Imperfect revisited: Exploring L1 influence in the reassembly of imperfective features onto new L2 forms. *Second Language Research* 33(4), 431–57.

Doughty, C. J . (2001). Cognitive underpinnings of focus on form. In P. Robinson (ed.), *Cognition and Second Language Instruction*, pp. 206–57. New York: Cambridge University Press.

Epstein, S., Flynn, S., and Martohardjono, G. (1996). Second language acquisition: Theoretical and experimental issues in contemporary research. *Brain and Behavioral Sciences*, 19, 677–758.

Escandell-Vidal, M. V. (2000). Categorías funcionales y semántica procedimental. In M. Martínez Hernández (ed.), *Cien años de investigación semántica. De Michel Breal a la actualidad*, pp. 363–78. Madrid: Ediciones Clásicas.

Escandell-Vidal, M. V. (2004). Norms and Principles. Putting social and cognitive pragmatics together. In R. Márquez-Reiter and M. E. Placencia (eds.), *Current Trends in the Pragmatics of Spanish*, pp. 347–72. Amsterdam: John Benjamins. https://doi.org/10.1075/pbns.123.27esc.

Escandell-Vidal, M. V. (2006). La teoría de la relevancia y sus implicaciones para la enseñanza de lenguas extranjeras. In J. Falk, J. Gille and F. Wachtmeister Bermúdez (eds.), *Discurso, interacción e identidad. Homenaje a Lars Fant*, pp. 231–54. Stockholm: Stockholm Universitet.

Escandell-Vidal, M. V. (2010). Futuro y evidencialidad. *Anuario de Lingüística Hispánica XXVI*, 9–34.

Escandell-Vidal, M. V. (2014). Evidential futures: The case of Spanish. In P. De Brabanter, M. Kissine and S. Sharifzadeh (eds.), *Future Times, Future Tenses*, pp. 219–247. Oxford: Oxford University Press.

Escandell-Vidal, M. V. (2016). Notes for a restrictive theory of procedural meaning. In R. Giora and M. Haugh (eds.), *Doing Pragmatics Interculturally*, pp. 79–96. Berlin: De Gruyter.

Escandell-Vidal, M. V. (2019a). El futuro del español. Sistema natural frente a usos cultivados. *Verba Hispánica* 26, 15–33.

Escandell-Vidal, M. V. (2019b). Evidential implicatures and mismatch resolution. In R. Carston, B. Clark and K. Scott (eds.), *Relevance, Pragmatics and Interpretation*, pp. 66–79. Cambridge: Cambridge University Press.

Escandell-Vidal, M. V. (2020). Léxico, pragmatica y comunicación lingüística. In M.V. Escandell, J. Amenós-Pons and A. Ahern (eds.), *Pragmática*, pp. 39–59. Madrid: Akal.

Escandell-Vidal, M. V. and M. Leonetti (2011). On the rigidity of procedural meaning. In M. V. Escandell-Vidal, M. Leonetti and A. Ahern (eds.), *Procedural Meaning: Problems and Perspectives*, pp. 81–102. Bingley: Emerald.

Escandell-Vidal, M. V. and M. Leonetti, (2012). El significado procedimental: rutas hacia una idea. In M. C. Horno and J. L. Mendívil (eds.), *La sabiduría de Mnemósine: Ensayos de historia de la lingüística ofrecidos a José Francisco Val Álvaro*, pp. 157–67. Zaragoza: Prensas Universitarias de Zaragoza.

Escandell-Vidal, V., Leonetti, M., and Ahern, A. (eds.) (2011). *Procedural Meaning: Problems and Perspectives*. Bingley: Emerald.

Escandell-Vidal, V. (2021). The semantics of the simple future in romance: Core meaning and parametric variation. In L. Baranzini and L. De Saussure (ed.), *Aspects of Tenses, Modality and Evidentiality*. Cahiers Chronos 31, 9–31. Amsterdam: Brill.

Escandell-Vidal, V. and Leonetti, M. (2002). Coercion and the stage / individual distinction. In J. Gutiérrez-Rexach (ed.), *From Words to Discourse: Trends in Spanish Semantics and Pragmatics*, pp. 159–80. Oxford: Elsevier.

Escandell-Vidal, V. and Leonetti, M. (2011). On the rigidity of procedural meaning. In V. Escandell-Vidal, M. Leonetti and A. Ahern (eds.), *Procedural Meaning: Problems and Perspectives*. Bingley: Emerald.

Figueras, C. (2020). La puntuación y el significado del texto. In M. V. Escandell, J. Amenós-Pons and A. Ahern (eds.), *Pragmática*, pp. 303–22. Madrid: Akal.

Fodor, J. A. (1983). *The Modularity of Mind*. Cambridge, MA: MIT Press.

Foster-Cohen, S. (2000). Relevance theory and language acquisition: A productive paradigm shift? *Bulletin of the International Association for the Study of Child Language* 20(1), 5–19.

Foster-Cohen, S. (2004). Relevance theory, action theory and second language communication strategies. *Second Language Research* 20(3), 289–302.

Garcés-Conejos, P. and Bou-Franch, P. (2004). A pragmatic account of listenership: Implications for foreign/second language teaching. *Revista Alicantina de Estudios Ingleses* 17, 81–102.

Gibbs, R. W. Jr. (2017). Experimental pragmatics. In Y. Huang (ed.), *The Oxford Handbook of Pragmatics,* pp. 310–26. Oxford University Press.

Goldberg, A. E. (1995). *Constructions: A Construction Grammar Approach to Argument Structure.* Chicago: University of Chicago Press.

González-Lloret, M. (2020). Pragmatic development in L2: An overview. In K. P. Schneider and E. Ifantidou (eds.), *Developmental and Clinical Pragmatics,* pp. 237–68. Berlin: De Gruyter.

Grice, H. P. (1975). Logic and Conversation. In P. Cole and J. Morgan (eds.), *Syntax and Semantics,* vol.3, pp. 41–58. New York: Academic Press.

Grinstead, J. (2004). Subjects and interface delay in child Spanish and Catalan. *Language,* 80 (1), 40–72.

Grisot, C. (2015). *Temporal Reference: Empirical and Theoretical Perspectives: Converging Evidence from English and Romance.* Geneva: University of Geneva.

Grisot, C. and J. Moeschler. (2014). How do empirical methods interact with theoretical pragmatics? The conceptual and procedural contents of the English simple past and its translation into French. In J. Romero-Trillo (ed.), *Yearbook of Corpus Linguistics and Pragmatics 2014: New Empirical and Theoretical Paradigms,* pp. 7–33. Cham: Springer.

Grisot. C. (2018). *Cohesion, Coherence and Temporal Reference from an Experimental Corpus Pragmatics Perspective.* Cham: Springer.

Guasti, M. T., Chierchia, G., Crain, S., Foppolo, F., Gualmini, A. and Meroni, L. (2005). Why children and adults sometimes (but not always) compute implicatures. *Language, Cognition and Neuroscience* 20(5), 667–96.

Guijarro-Fuentes, P. and Rothman, J. (eds.) (2012). Interfaces in child language acquisition: Special issue. *First Language* 32(1– 2).

Guijarro-Fuentes, P., Ahern, A., and Amenós-Pons, J. (2020). La interfaz gramática/pragmática y su papel en el aprendizaje de segundas lenguas. In V. Escandell-Vidal, J. Amenós Pons and A. Ahern (eds.), *Pragmática,* pp. 713–28. Madrid: Akal.

Guijarro-Fuentes, P. and Pires, A. (2023). Feature acquisition: Object drop in L2 Spanish. *Probus* 35(2), 251–275.

Happé, F., Cook, J. L. and Bird, G. (2017). The structure of social cognition: In(ter)dependence of sociocognitive processes. *Annual Review of Psychology* 68, 243–267

Hawkins, R. and Chan, C. (1997). The partial availability of Universal Grammar in second language acquisition: The 'failed functional features hypothesis'. *Second Language Research* 13, 187–226.

Hawkins, R. and Franceschina, F. (2004). Explaining the acquisition of and non acquisition of determiner-noun gender concord in French and Spanish. In

P. Prévost and J. Paradis (eds.), *The Acquisition of French in Different Contexts: Focus on Functional Categories*, pp. 175–205. Amsterdam: John Benjamins.

Hawkins, R. and Hattori, H. (2006). Interpretation of English multiple *wh*-questions by Japanese speakers: A missing uninterpretable feature account. *Second Language Research* 22, 269–301

Hoff, H. E. (2020). The evolution of intercultural communicative competence: conceptualisations, critiques and consequences for 21st century classroom practice. *Intercultural Communication Education* 3(2), 55–74.

Horn, L. (1984). Toward a new taxonomy for pragmatic inference: Q-based and R-based implicature. In D. Schiffrin (ed.), *Meaning, Form and Text in Context: Linguistic Applications*, pp. 11–42. Washington, DC: Georgetown University Press.

Horn, L. (1989). *A Natural History of Negation*. Chicago: University of Chicago Press.

Horn, L. (2004). Implicature. In L. R. Horn and G. Ward (eds.), *The Handbook of Pragmatics*, pp. 3–28. Oxford: Blackwell.

Hyams, N. (1992). A reanalysis of null subjects in child language. In J. Weissenborn, H. Goodluck, and T. Roeper (eds.), *Theoretical Issues in Language Acquisition: Continuity and Change in Development*, pp. 249–67. New York: Lawrence Erlbaum.

Ifantidou, E. (2014). *Pragmatic Competence and Relevance*. Amsterdam: John Benjamins.

Ifantidou, E. (2022). Pragmatic competence. In I. Kecskes (ed.), *The Cambridge Handbook of Intercultural Pragmatics*, pp. 741–64. Cambridge: Cambridge University Press.

Jackendoff, R. (1997). *The Architecture of the Language Faculty*. Cambridge, MA: MIT Press.

Jackendoff, R. (2002). *Foundations of Language: Brain, Meaning, Grammar, Evolution*. New York: Oxford University Press.

Kasper, G. (2006). Speech acts in interaction: Towards discursive pragmatics. In K. Bardori-Harlig, C. Félix-Brasdefer, and A. Omar (eds.), *Pragmatics and Language Learning*, pp. 281–314. National Foreign Language Resource Center, University of Hawai'i at Mānoa, Honolulu.

Kasper, G. and Rose, K. R. (2002). Pragmatic development in a second language. *Language Learning* 52 (Suppl. 1), 1–352.

Katsos, N. y Bishop, D. V. M. (2011). Pragmatic Tolerance: Implications for the acquisition of informativeness and implicature. *Cognition* 120, 67–81.

Kecskes, I. (2014). *Intercultural Pragmatics*. Oxford: Oxford University Press.

Kecskes, I. (2016). Can intercultural pragmatics bring some new insight into pragmatic theories? In A. Capone, and J. L. Mey (eds.), *Interdisciplinary Studies in Pragmatics, Culture and Society*, pp. 43–71. Cham: Springer.

Kolaiti, P. and Wilson, D. (2014). Corpus analysis and lexical pragmatics: An overview. *International Review of Pragmatics* 6, 211–39.

Kövecses, Z. (2006). *Language, Mind and Culture*. Oxford: Oxford University Press.

Langacker R. W. (1987). *Foundation of Cognitive Grammar (Vol. 1). Theoretical Prerequisites*. Stanford: Stanford University Press.

Langacker, R. W. (1991). *Foundations of Cognitive Grammar (Vol. 2). Descriptive Application*. Stanford: Stanford University Press.

Lardiere, D. (2009). Some thoughts on the contrastive analysis of features in second language acquisition. *Second Language Research* 25, 171–225.

Lardiere, L. (2008). Feature-assembly in second language acquisition. In J. Liceras, H. Zobl and H. Goodluck (eds.), The role of formal features in second language acquisition, pp. 106–40. New York: Lawrence Erlbaum Associates.

Le Querler, N. (1996). *Typologie des modalités*. Caen: Presses Universitaires de Caen.

Lenneberg, E. (1967). *Biological Foundations of Language*. New York: John Wiley and Sons.

Leonetti, M. (2004). Specificity and differential object marking in Spanish. *Catalan Journal of Linguistics* 3(1), 75–114.

Leonetti, M. (2007). Clitics do not encode specificity. In G. Kaiser and M. Leonetti (eds.), *Proceedings of the Workshop «Definiteness, Specificity and Animacy in Ibero-Romance Languages», Arbeitspapier – Fachbereich Sprachwissenschaft der Universität Konstanz*, pp. 111–39. Konstanz: University of Konstanz.

Leonetti, M. and Escandell-Vidal, V. (2003). On the quotative readings of Spanish imperfecto. *Cuadernos de Lingüística* 10, 135–154.

Levelt, W. J. M. (ed.). (1993). *Lexical Access in Speech Production*. Cambridge, MA: Blackwell.

Levinson, S. C. (1987a). Minimization and conversational inference. In J. Verschueren and M. Bertucceli-Papi (eds.), *The Pragmatics Perspective*, pp. 61–129. Amsterdam: John Benjamins.

Levinson, S. C. (1987b). Pragmatics and the grammar of anaphora. *Journal of Linguistics* 23, 379–434.

Levinson, S. C. (1991). Pragmatic reductions of the binding conditions revisited. *Journal of Linguistics* 27, 107–61.

Levinson, S. C. (1995). Three levels of meaning. In F. R. Palmer (ed.), *Grammar and Meaning*, pp. 90–115. Cambridge: Cambridge University Press.

Levinson, S. C. (2000). *Presumptive Meanings: The Theory of Generalized Conversational Implicature*. Cambridge, MA: MIT Press.

Liceras, J. M. (1996). *La adquisición de las lenguas segundas y la gramática universal*. Madrid, Síntesis.

Liszka, S. (2004). Exploring the effects of first language influence on second language pragmatic processes from a syntactic deficit perspective. *Second Language Research* 20(3), 213–31.

LoCastro, V. (2003). *An Introduction to Pragmatics: Social Action for Language Teachers*. Ann Arbor, Michigan: The University of Michigan Press.

Long, M. (2014). *Second Language Acquisition and Task-Based Language Teaching*. Oxford: Wiley-Blackwell.

Loureda, O., Cruz, A., Recio, I., and Rudka, M. (2021). *Comunicación, cognición y pragmática experimental*. Madrid: Arco Libros.

Lozano, C. (2006a). Focus and split intransitivity: The acquisition of word order alternations in non-native Spanish. *Second Language Research* 22, 1–43.

Lozano, C. (2006b). The development of syntax-discourse interface: Greek learners of Spanish. In V. Torrens and L. Escobar (eds.), *The Acquisition of Syntax in Romance Languages*, pp. 371–99. Amsterdam: John Benjamins.

Marsden H. (2009). Distributive quantifier scope in English–Japanese and Korean–Japanese interlanguage. *Language Acquisition*, 16, 135–77.

Mazzarella, D. (2013). Optimal relevance as a pragmatic criterion: the role of epistemic vigilance. *University College Working Papers in Linguistics* 25, 20–45.

Mercier, H. and Sperber, D. (2011) Why do humans reason? Arguments for an argumentative theory. *Behavioral and Brain Sciences* 34(2), 94–111.

Mercier, H. and Sperber, D. (2017). *The Enigma of Reason*. Cambridge, MA: Harvard University Press.

Mercier, H. and Sperber, D. (2019). Précis of *The Enigma of Reason*. *Teorema* 38(1), 69–76.

Moens, M. and Steedman, M. (1988). Temporal ontology and temporal reference. *Computational Linguistics* 14(2), 15–28.

Moeschler, J. (1998a). Ordre temporel, causalité et relations de discours: une approche pragmatique. In S. Vogeleer, A. Borillo, C. Vetters, and M. Vuillaume (eds.), *Temps et discours*, pp. 45–64. Louvain-la-Neuve: Peeters.

Moeschler, J. (1998b). Pragmatique de la référence temporelle. In J. Moeschler, J. Jayez, M. Kozlowska, et al. (eds.), Le temps des événements, pp. 157–80. Paris: Kimé.

Moeschler, J. (2000a). Le modèle des inférences directionnelles. *Cahiers de Linguistique Française*, 22, 57–100.

Moeschler, J. (2000b). L'ordre temporel est-il naturel? In J. Moeschler and M.-J. Béguelin (eds.), *Référence temporelle et nominale*, pp. 71–105. Berne: Peter Lang.

Moeschler, J. (2015). Argumentation and connectives. In A. Capone and J. L. Mey (eds.), *Interdisciplinary Studies in Pragmatics, Culture and Society, Perspectives in Pragmatics*, pp. 405–36. Cham: Springer.

Moeschler, J. (2016). Where is procedural meaning located? Evidence from discourse connectives and tenses. *Lingua* 175, 122–38.

Moeschler, J. (2019). *Non-Lexical Pragmatics. Time, Causality, and Logical Words*. Berlin: De Gruyter.

Moeschler, J., Grisot, C., and Cartoni, B. (2012). Jusqu'où les temps verbaux sont-ils procéduraux? *Nouveaux Cahiers de Linguistique Française* 30, 119–39.

Montrul, S. (2002). Incomplete acquisition and attrition of Spanish tense/aspect distinctions in adult bilinguals. *Bilingualism: Language and Cognition* 5, 39–68.

Montrul, S. (2004). Subject and object expression in Spanish heritage speakers: A case of morpho-syntactic convergence. *Bilingualism: Language and Cognition* 7, 125–42.

Müller, N. and Hulk, D. (2001). Crosslinguistic influence in bilingual language acquisition: Italian and French as recipient languages. *Bilingualism: Language and Cognition* 4, 1–21.

Nizegorodcew, A. (2007). *Input for Instructed L2 Learners. The Relevance of Relevance*. Bristol: Multilingual Matters.

Noveck, I. (2018). *Experimental Pragmatics: The Making of a Cognitive Science*. Cambridge: Cambridge University Press.

Noveck, I. A. and Posada, A. (2003). Characterizing the time course of an implicature: An evoked potentials study. *Brain and Language* 85, 203–10.

Noveck, I. and Sperber, D. (eds.) (2004). *Experimental Pragmatics*. London: Palgrave.

O'Grady, W. (2005b). S*yntactic Carpentry: An Emergentist Approach to Syntax*. Mahah, NJ: Erlbaum.

O'Grady, W. (2005a). *How Children Learn Language*. Cambridge, Cambridge University Press.

Origgi, G. and Sperber, D. (2000). Evolution, communication, and the proper function of language. In P. Carruthers and A. Chamberlain (eds.), *Evolution and the Human Mind: Language, Modularity and Social Cognition*, pp. 140–69. Cambridge: Cambridge University Press.

Paiva, B.-M. (2003). Pragmatic interaction in a second language. In C. Grant (ed.), *Rethinking Communicative Interaction. New Interdisciplinary Horizons*, pp. 187–206. Amsterdam, Philadelphia: John Benjamins.

Paiva, B.-M. and Foster-Cohen, S. (2004). Exploring the relationships between theories of second language acquisition and relevance theory. *Second Language Research* 20(3), 281–8.

Papafragou, A. and Tantalou, N. (2004). Children's computation of implicatures. *Language Acquisition* 12(1), 71–82.

Paradis, J. and Navarro, S. (2003). Subject realization and crosslinguistic interference in the bilingual acquisition of Spanish and English: What is the role of the input? *Journal of Child Language* 30(2), 371–90.

Perez Saldanya, M. (2008). Les relacions temporals i aspectuals. In J. Solà (dir.), M. R. Lloret, J. Mascaró and M. Pérez-Saldanya (eds.), *Gramàtica del català contemporani*, vol. 3, 2567–662. Barcelona: Empúries.

Pinker, S. (2007). *The Language Instinct*. New York: Harper Perennial Modern Classics.

Pouscoulous, N. (2013). Early pragmatics with words. In F. Liedtke and C. Schulze (eds.), *Beyond Words. Content, Context and Inference*, pp. 121–144. Berlin: Mouton.

Rastelli, S. (2023). Noncombinatorial grammar: A challenge for memory research on second language acquisition and bilingualism. *Journal of Neurolinguistics* 65, 1–16. https://doi.org/10.1016/j.jneuroling.2022.101112.

Rasuki, M. (2017). Processing instruction: A review of issues. *International Journal of Education and Literacy Studies* 5(3), 1–7.

Reboul, A. (2015). Why language really is not a communication system: A cognitive view of language evolution. *Frontiers in Psychology* 6, 1–12.

Reboul, A. (2017). *Cognition and Communication in the Evolution of Language*. Oxford, Oxford University Press.

Recio Fernández, I. (2020). *The Impact of Procedural Meaning on Second Language Processing: A Study on Connectives*. PhD dissertation. Heidelberg: University of Heidelberg.

Rice, M. L. Wexler, K. and Hershberger, S. (1998). Tense over time: The longitudinal course of tense acquisition in children with specific language impairment. *Journal of Speech, Language, and Hearing Research* 41(6), 1412–31.

Risager, K. (2018) *Representations of the World in Language Textbooks.* Bristol: Multilingual Matters.

Rocci, A. (2000). L'interprétation épistemique du futur en italien et en français: une analyse procédurale. *Cahiers de linguistique française* 22, 241–74.

Rose, K. R. and G. Kasper (2001). *Pragmatics in Language Teaching.* Cambridge: Cambridge University Press.

Schachter, J. (1989). Testing a proposed universal. In S. Gass and J. Schachter (eds.), *Linguistic perspectives on Second Language Acquisition*, pp. 73–88. Cambridge: Cambridge University Press.

Schaden, G. (2009a). Present perfects compete. *Linguistics and Philosophy* 32(2), 115–41.

Schaden, G. (2009b). *Composés et surcomposés: Le 'parfait' en français, allemand, anglais et espagnol.* Paris: L'Harmattan.

Schmid. H.-J. (2012). Generalising the apparently ungeneralizable: Basic ingredients of a cognitive-pragmatic approach to the construal of meaning-in-context. In H.-J. Schmid (ed.), *Cognitive Pragmatics*, pp. 3–22. Berlin: De Gruyter.

Schwartz, B. D. and Sprouse, R. A. (1996). L2 cognitive states and the full transfer/full access model. *Second Language Research* 12, 40–72.

Scott, K., Clark, B., and Carston, R. (2019). *Relevance, Pragmatics and Interpretation.* Cambridge: Cambridge University Press.

Scott-Phillips, T. (2015). *Speaking Our Minds: Why Human Communication is Different, and How Language Evolved to Make it Special.* Basingstoke: Palgrave Macmillan.

Searle, J. R. (1969). *Speech Acts: An Essay in the Philosophy of Language.* Cambridge: Cambridge University Press.

Searle, J. R. (1972). Speech acts: An essay in the philosophy of language. *Mind* 81(323), 458–68.

Serratrice, L., Sorace, A., and Paoli, S. 2004. Transfer at the syntax-pragmatics interface: Subjects and objects in Italian-English bilingual and monolingual acquisition. *Bilingualism: Language and Cognition* 7, 183–205.

Sharwood Smith, M. and Truscott, J. (2014). *The Multilingual Mind: A Modular Processing Perspective.* Cambridge: Cambridge University Press.

Sharwood-Smith, M. (2017). *Introducing Language and Cognition.* Oxford: Oxford University Press.

Sharwood Smith, M. (2021a). Language transfer: A useful or pernicious concept? *Second Language Research* 37(3), 409–14.

Sharwood Smith, M. (2021b). The cognitive status of metalinguistic knowledge in speakers of one or more languages. *Bilingualism Language and Cognition* 24, 185–96.

Slabakova, R. (2006). Is there a critical period for the acquisition of semantics? *Second Language Research* 22, 302–38.

Slabakova, R. (2008). *Meaning in the Second Language*. Berlin: Mouton de Gruyter.

Slabakova, R., Leal, T. and Liskin-Gasparro, J. (2014). We have moved on: Current concepts and positions in generative SLA. *Applied Linguistics*, 35, 601–6.

Smith, N. and Tsimpli, I. M. (1995). *The Mind of a Savant: Language Learning and Modularity*. Oxford: Basil Blackwell.

Smith, N., Tsimpli, I., Morgan, G. and Woll, B. (2011). *The Signs of a Savant: Language against the Odds*. Cambridge: Cambridge University Press.

Sorace, A. (2004). Native language attrition and developmental instability at the syntax-discourse interface: Data, interpretations and methods. *Bilingualism: Language and Cognition* 7, 143–5.

Sorace, A. (2005). Selective optionality in language development. In L. Cornips and K. P. Corrigan (eds.), *Syntax and Variation: Reconciling the Biological and the Social*, pp. 55–80. Amsterdam: John Benjamins.

Sorace, A. (2006). Possible manifestations of shallow processing in advanced second language speakers. *Applied Psycholinguistics* 27, 88–91.

Sorace, A. (2011). Pinning down the concept of 'interface' in bilingualism. *Linguistic Approaches to Bilingualism* 1(1), 1–33.

Sorace, A. (2012). Pinning down the concept of interface in bilingualism: A reply to peer commentaries. *Linguistic Approaches to Bilingualism* 2–2, 209–16.

Sorace, A. and Filiaci, F. (2006). Anaphora resolution in near-native speakers of Italian. *Second Language Research* 22, 339–68.

Soria, B. and Romero, E. (eds.) (2010). *Explicit Communication: Robyn Carston's Pragmatics*. New York: Palgrave/MacMillan.

Sperber, D. (1994). The modularity of thought and the epidemiology of representations. In L. A. Hirschfeld and S. A. Gelman (eds.), *Mapping the Mind: Domain Specificity in Cognition and Culture*, pp. 39–67. Cambridge: Cambridge University Press.

Sperber, D. (1994). Understanding verbal understanding. In J. Khalfa (ed.), *What is Intelligence?* pp. 179–98. Cambridge: Cambridge University Press.

Sperber, D. (1996). *Explaining Culture: A Naturalistic Approach*. Oxford: Blackwell.

Sperber, D. (2000). Metarepresentations in an evolutionary perspective. In D. Sperber (ed.), *Metarepresentations: A Multidisciplinary Perspective*, pp. 117–37. Oxford: Oxford University Press.

Sperber, D. (2005). Modularity and relevance: How can a massively modular mind be flexible and context-sensitive? In P. Carruthers, S. Laurence, and S. Stich (eds.), *The Innate Mind: Structure and Content*, pp. 53–68. Oxford: Oxford University Press.

Sperber, D. (2006). Why a deep understanding of cultural evolution is incompatible with shallow psychology. In N. Enfield and S. Levinson (eds.), *Roots of Human Sociality*, pp. 431–49. London: Bloomsbury.

Sperber, D. and D. Wilson (1986/1995). *Relevance: Communication and Cognition*. Oxford: Blackwell.

Sperber, D. and D. Wilson (1987). Précis of relevance communication and cognition. *Behavioral and Brain Sciences* 10, 697–754.

Sperber, D. and Wilson, D. (1998). The mapping between the mental and the public lexicon. In P. Carruthers and J. Boucher (eds.), *Thought and Language*, pp. 184–200. Cambridge: Cambridge University Press.

Sperber, D. and D. Wilson (2002). Pragmatics, modularity and mind-reading. *Mind and Language 17*, 3–23.

Sperber, D. and D. Wilson (2005). Pragmatics. In F. Jackson and M. Smith (eds.), *Oxford Handbook of Philosophy of Language*, pp. 468–501. Oxford: Oxford University Press.

Sperber, D., Clément, F., Heintz, C., et al. (2010). Epistemic vigilance. *Mind and Language 25*(4), 359–93.

Sportiche, D. (1996). Clitic constructions. In J. Rooryck and Zaring, L. (eds.), *Phrase Structure and the Lexicon. Studies in Natural Language and Linguistic Theory*, vol. 33, pp. 213–66.Dordrecht: Springer.

Suñer, M. (1988). The role of agreement in clitic-doubled constructions. *Natural Language and Linguistic Theory* 6(3), 391–434.

Svenonius, P. (2021). Prepositions with CP and their implications for extended projections. *Linguistic Variation* 21(1), 11–45.

Tasmowski, L. and Dendale, P. (1998). Must/will and doit/futur simple as epistemic modal markers. Semantic value and restrictions of use. In J. E. van der Auwera (ed.), *English as a Human Language: To honour Louis Goossens*, pp. 325–36. Munich: Lincom Europa.

Taguchi, N. (ed.) (2019). *The Routledge Handbook of Second Language Acquisition and Pragmatics*. New York: Taylor and Francis.

Taguchi, N. and Roever, C. (2017). *Second Language Pragmatics*. Oxford: Oxford University Press.

Tomasello, M. (2003). *Constructing a Language: A Usage-Based Theory of Language Acquisition*. Cambridge, MA: Harvard University Press.

Tomasello, M. (2008). *Origins of Human Communication*. Cambridge, MA: MIT Press.

Truscott, J. (2015). *Consciousness and Second Language Learning*. Clevedon: Multilingual Matters.

Truscott, J. (2022). *Working Memory in the Modular Mind*. New York: Routledge.

Truscott, J. and Sharwood-Smith, M. (2019). *The Internal Context of Bilingual Processing and Acquisition*. Amsterdam: John Benjamins.

Tsimpli, I. M. and Dimitrakopoulou, M. (2007). The interpretability hypothesis: Evidence from *wh* -interrogatives in second language acquisition. *Second Language Research, 23*, 215–42.

Tsimpli, I. M. and Sorace, A. (2006). Differentiating interfaces: L2 performance in syntax-semantics and syntax-discourse phenomena. In D. Bamman, T. Magnitskaia, and C. Zaller (eds.), *Proceedings of the 30th Boston University Conference on Language Development*, pp. 653–64. Somerville, MA: Cascadilla Press.

Tsimpli, I.-M., Sorace, A., Heycock, C. and Filiaci, F. (2004). First language attrition and syntactic subjects: A study of Greek and Italian near-native speakers of English. *International Journal of Bilingualism* 8, 257–77.

Tsimpli. I.-M. and Mastropavlou, M. (2008). Feature interpretability in L2 acquisition and SLI: Greek clitics and determiners. In J. H. Liceras and H. Goodluck (eds.), *The Role of Formal Features in Second Language Acquisition*, pp. 143–83. Mahwah, NJ: Erlbaum.

Ullman, M. (2016). The declarative/procedural model: A neurobiological model of language learning, knowledge, and use. In G. Hickok, S. Small (eds.), *Neurobiology of Language*, pp. 953–68. Elsevier: Amsterdam.

VanPatten, B. (1996). *Input Processing and Grammar Instruction: Theory and Research*. Norwood, NJ: Ablex.

VanPatten, B. (2007). Input processing in adult SLA. IIn B. VanPatten and J. Williams (eds.), *Theories in Second Language Acquisition: An Introduction*, pp. 115–35. Mahwah, NJ: Erlbaum.

VanPatten, B. (ed). (2004). *Processing Instruction: Theory, Research and Commentary*. Mahwah, NJ: Erlbaum.

VanPatten, B. and Smith, M. (2022). *Explicit and Implicit Learning in Second Language Acquisition*. Cambridge: Cambridge University Press.

VanPatten, B., Smith, M. and Benati, A. (2020). *Key Questions in Second Language Acquisition*. Cambridge: Cambridge University Press.

Wexler, K. (1998). Very early parameter setting and the unique checking constraint: A new explanation of the optional infinitive stage. *Lingua.* 106 (1–4), 23–79.

Wharton, T. (2016). That bloody so-and-so has retired: Expressives revisited. *Lingua*, 175, 20–3.

White, L. (1989). *Universal Grammar and Second Language Acquisition.* Amsterdam: John Benjamins.

White, L. (2003). *Second Language Acquisition and Universal Grammar.* New York: Cambridge University Press.

White, L. (2009). Grammatical theory: Interfaces and L2 knowledge. In W. C. Ritchie and T. K. Bhatia (eds.), *The New Handbook of Second Language Acquisition*, pp. 49–68. Leiden: Brill.

Wigger, L.-G. (2005). *Die Entwicklungsgeschichte der romanischen Vergangenheitstempora am Beispiel des Pretérito Perfeito Composto im Portugiesischen.* Tübingen: University of Tübingen.

Wilson, D. (2000/2012). Metarepresentation in linguistic communication. In D. Sperber and D. Wilson (eds.), *Meaning and Relevance*, 123–145. Cambridge: Cambridge University Press.

Wilson, D. (2005). New directions for research on pragmatics and modularity. *Lingua* 115(8), 1129–46.

Wilson, D. (2011). The conceptual-procedural distinction: Past, present and future. In V. Escandell-Vidal, M. Leonetti, M and A. Ahern (eds.), *Procedural Meaning: Problems and Perspectives*, pp. 3–31. Bingley: Emerald.

Wilson, D. (2016). Reassessing the conceptual–procedural distinction. *Lingua* 175–6, 5–19.

Wilson, D. (2016). Relevance theory. In Y. Huang (ed.), *Oxford Handbook of Pragmatics*, pp. 79–100. Oxford: Oxford University Press.

Wilson, D. (2017). Relevance theory. In Y. Huang (ed.), *The Oxford Handbook of Pragmatics*, pp. 79–100. Oxford, Oxford University Press.

Wilson, D. and Carston, R. (2007). A unitary approach to lexical pragmatics: Relevance, inference and ad hoc concepts. In N. Burton-Roberts (ed.), *Pragmatics*, pp. 230–60. Basingstoke: Palgrave Macmillan.

Wilson, D. and Sperber, D. (1993). Linguistic form and relevance. *Lingua 90*, 1–25.

Wilson, D. and Sperber, D. (2004). Relevance Theory. In L. R. Horn and G. Ward (eds.), *The Handbook of Pragmatics*, pp. 607–32. Oxford: Blackwell.

Wilson, D. and Sperber, D. (2012). *Meaning and Relevance.* Cambridge: Cambridge University Press.

Zufferey, S. (2010). *Lexical Pragmatics and Theory of Mind.* Amsterdam/ Philadelphia: John Benjamins.

Zufferey, S. (2015). *Acquiring Pragmatics: Social and Cognitive Perspectives.* New York: Routledge.

Zufferey, S. (2020). Pragmatic development in L1. An overview. In K.P. Schneider and W. Ifantidou, *Developmental and Clinical Pragmatics,* pp. 33–60. Berlin: De Gruyter.

Acknowledgements

We are grateful to our research colleagues and the funding bodies, including the Spanish Ministry for Science and Innovation, which made it possible for us to write this Element. We also thank the series editors for their helpful guidance, and the anonymous reviewers for the intelligent, thoughtful remarks and suggestions on the first draft of the manuscript.

Cambridge Elements

Second Language Acquisition

Alessandro G. Benati

University College Dublin

Alessandro G. Benati is Professor and Head of the School of Education at University College Dublin. He is visiting and honorary professor at the University of York St. John, Anaheim and the University of Hong Kong. Alessandro is known for his work in second language acquisition and second language teaching. He has published ground-breaking research on the pedagogical framework called Processing Instruction.

John W. Schwieter

Wilfrid Laurier University, Ontario

John W. Schwieter is Associate Professor of Spanish and Linguistics, and Faculty of Arts Teaching Scholar, at Wilfrid Laurier University. His research interests include psycholinguistic and neurolinguistic approaches to multilingualism and language acquisition; second language teaching and learning; translation and cognition; and language, culture, and society.

About the Series

Second Language Acquisition showcases a high-quality set of updatable, concise works that address how learners come to internalize the linguistic system of another language and how they make use of that linguistic system. Contributions reflect the interdisciplinary nature of the field, drawing on theories, hypotheses, and frameworks from education, linguistics, psychology, and neurology, among other disciplines. Each Element in this series addresses several important questions: What are the key concepts?; What are the main branches of research?; What are the implications for SLA?; What are the implications for pedagogy?; What are the new avenues for research?; and What are the key readings?

Cambridge Elements ☰

Second Language Acquisition

Elements in the Series

Printed in the United States
by Baker & Taylor Publisher Services